The Royal Homes in Gloucestershire

The Royal Homes in Gloucestershire

HIGHGROVE · GATCOMBE PARK · NETHER LYPIATT

Geoffrey Sanders and
David Verey

FOREWORD BY
Rosemary Verey

PHOTOGRAPHS BY
Paul Felix

EDITOR
Siân Ellis

ALAN SUTTON

First published in the United Kingdom in 1992

Alan Sutton Publishing Ltd

Phoenix Mill · Far Thrupp · Stroud · Gloucestershire

First published in the United States of America in 1992

Alan Sutton Publishing Inc · Wolfeboro Falls · NH 03896–0848

Foreword and Garden Features copyright © Rosemary Verey, 1992

Highgrove colour photographs by Paul Felix copyright © A.G. Carrick
 Ltd, 1992

Text and this edition copyright © Alan Sutton Publishing, 1992

British Library Cataloguing in Publication Data

Verey, Rosemary
 The royal homes in Gloucestershire. – Rev. ed
 I. Title II. Verey, David, *1913–1984*
 III. Sanders, Geoffrey
 942.417

ISBN 0–7509–0078–4 (case)
ISBN 0–7509–0145–4 (paper)

Library of Congress Cataloging in Publication Data applied for

Half-title illustration: one of Highgrove's 'royal' lamps
Frontispiece: a window in a yew hedge reveals a quiet corner of the rose
garden at Highgrove

Typeset in 11/17 Baskerville.
Typesetting and origination by Alan Sutton Publishing Limited.
Colour separation by Yeo Graphics, Wells.
Printed in Great Britain by Bath Press Colourbooks Ltd, Glasgow.

Contents

Foreword

BY ROSEMARY VEREY

It is my privilege to contribute to the new edition of *The Royal Homes in Gloucestershire*. The authors of this small book, my husband David Verey and Geoffrey Sanders, sadly have both died, and a decade has passed since its publication. I believe that an even greater affection is now felt in our county towards the three royal families, and a pride that they chose the Cotswolds for their country homes. The Princess Royal (then Princess Anne) has lived at Gatcombe Park since 1976. The Prince of Wales came to Highgrove in 1980, and the same year Prince and Princess Michael of Kent bought Nether Lypiatt.

The Prince of Wales arrived as a bachelor in Gloucestershire – an ideal county for an enthusiastic young man loving country pursuits, and with beautiful unspoilt surroundings. Here, near Tetbury, he is close to much of the land belonging to the Duchy of Cornwall.

There was great rejoicing in 1981 when he married the young and beautiful Lady Diana Spencer and brought her to share his country home. Together they have revitalized the house, both inside and out. The Prince's eye for proportion and detail is evident in the façade of the house, which has

A family photograph amidst the wild flowers in front of Highgrove. The façade has been extensively renovated since this picture was taken – just one instance of the many ways in which the Prince and Princess of Wales have revitalized this Cotswold house

been given a new stature and importance, and the garden is evolving as a garden should, with new trees, new borders, new thoughts. He has made his own mark on house, garden and estate.

A home is incomplete without a family and now their young sons, Prince William, born in 1982, and Prince Harry, born in 1984, are the right age to enjoy the freedom of their surroundings – galloping ponies, riding bicycles and climbing trees. They are boys full of fun and independent spirit, learning about the country matters which, by teaching and instinct, have been passed on to generations of Gloucestershire boys. These moments of freedom and privacy are so important for all the royal family.

Highgrove House is surrounded by 170 acres of parkland, with additional farmland in the immediate vicinity. HRH loves and personally supervises this estate, and it amazes me how he has an eye for every detail when his public life involves him in a multitude of activities touching so many people. The Prince and his wife are increasingly aware of the needs of others, in the business world where opportunity now falters, and in the world of the underprivileged and handicapped. We are fortunate to have as our future monarch a man who understands the problems and aspirations of the people, especially those who, through lack of finance or dreariness of surroundings, may never have the opportunity to realize their dreams. At the same time, he is setting an example in organic farming, and on a wider spectrum has an absorbing interest in caring for the countryside and the future of our environment.

The life cycle of most old houses includes good times and moments when they become run down. Nether Lypiatt is a typical example, and the imagination, energy and determination of Prince and Princess Michael of Kent have wrought wonders in the way they have restored this magical house. For three years from 1977 they longed to own the manor, with its charming character and similarity to that perfect 'doll's house' Ashdown Park in Berkshire, and to restore it to the splendour that was its due. There were rumours of ghosts, especially unfriendly to women, but when the princess walked into the cold hall for the first time she felt an unseen hand drape an invisible shawl about her shoulders, a gesture of welcome and a sensation of warmth in the house which she has felt ever since. That day it was nettle soup for lunch – nettles had taken over the garden, annihilating plants and hiding structures previously brought to perfection by garden lovers, especially by Lord Barrington. Now it became the turn of Prince and Princess Michael to wave their wand.

The inside of the house was filled with more light as blocked windows were opened up. Entering the front door up a flight of steps on the west side, you are immediately in the *piano nobile*, but as the house is built on sloping ground the east façade has an extra lower storey, and in consequence a more perfect architectural proportion. The tall first floor window on this side led into space, and this has now been given a balcony. A door was made from the dining-room into the garden on this same side, but it was cleverly disguised to preserve the symmetry of the façade.

In the garden existing features, such as the mature yew hedges, the wonderful avenue of limes and the wrought-iron gate and railings, have all been carefully nurtured and their importance enhanced. There is much new planting, all in keeping with the spirit of this elegant fairy-tale home.

The house at Gatcombe Park is beautifully sited, nestling

gently beside a wooded hillside. All the main rooms on the south façade command views down an intimate, unspoilt valley, and the architectural beauty of the house is in perfect accord with the natural beauty of the vista. There are no other houses in sight; beech trees and rolling grass meadows dominate the landscape, and on either side rise hills too steep to plough.

This view could haunt me with its stillness, its pervading feeling of permanence – it is not necessary to plan an elaborate garden when there is such an amazing natural setting, with pheasants honking, honey-coloured quoin stones, ivy clambering and old indigenous trees. To me, Gatcombe is the perfect example where man should not interfere with nature.

Introduction

Highgrove, Gatcombe Park and Nether Lypiatt are set only a few miles apart on the south-western edge of the Cotswolds. They have always been notable estates in Gloucestershire as the homes of the gentry and well-to-do, and each is of historic and architectural interest in its own right. For more than a decade now, though, they have been the subject of particular attention as the homes of members of the royal family – and as such they have firmly established in the public mind Gloucestershire's links with royalty.

Such links have not just existed in modern times, however, but can be traced back to the period of the Saxons. By the middle of the seventh century the country was divided into several small kingdoms, the largest of which, Mercia, included Gloucestershire. One of the most important cities of Mercia was Winchcombe and there was once a royal palace there. Cirencester, too, had its castle, built somewhat later, in which King Canute held a council in AD 1020. Nothing remains today because Stephen demolished the castle in the twelfth century.

The title of the *Royal* Forest of Dean originates from Canute's time. Holding court at Winchester, he command-ed that a part of west Gloucestershire should become the

king's hunting ground and he created special courts and officials to carry out the administration of the land there, its deer, timber and mineral rights. The forest was later adopted by Norman and Plantagenet kings as a favoured hunting ground, and ever since the area has enjoyed a very particular status as a community rather apart from the rest of Gloucestershire.

Edward the Confessor, who came to the throne in 1042, established Gloucester as the place for his councils and courts, and after the Conquest William I made a tradition of keeping Christmas at Gloucester and held his Parliament there. It was from Gloucester in the year 1085, after William had been in deep discussions with his councillors, that the order went out for the compilation of the 'Domesday Book'.

Gloucester continued as a centre of national importance when King John, William's great-great-grandson, died in 1216 and his son was hurriedly crowned at St Peter's Abbey, Gloucester as Henry III. The coronation was performed, so it is said, using a bracelet belonging to Henry's mother because King John had lost the crown jewels in the Wash.

A century later, Gloucester was the venue not for royal celebration but for the funeral of the murdered Edward II, Henry's grandson. Edward had become unpopular and many of his barons and his own queen Isabella rose against him. Deposed, he was kept a prisoner, finally being taken to Berkeley Castle in the summer of 1327. It was thought that because of his physical weakness Edward would not survive the insalubrious conditions of his captivity, but he did, and in the end he was murdered (20 September 1327). Fearful of the barons who had overthrown Edward, no abbot would give the former king's body burial – until the brave Abbot Thokey of Gloucester came to Berkeley and demanded to be

Berkeley Castle, grim residence of Edward II during his last summer of captivity. Here he was brutally murdered in 1327

13

allowed to take away the corpse. Edward II was subsequently buried at St Peter's, his queen and son Edward III coming to Gloucester for the state funeral in December 1327. Thokey's daring act was soon acknowledged with gratitude because when people realized the new king was no better than the old they regretted the murder. Consequently many were glad to be able to pay homage to the shrine of Edward II which had been created on the north side of St Peter's choir.

In the later Middle Ages the three Yorkist brothers, Edward IV, George, Duke of Clarence and Richard, Duke of Gloucester, had quite strong links with the county, and during the rising which aimed to restore Henry VI to the throne Gloucester played a key role in determining the outcome of events. Henry's queen, Margaret of Anjou, stopped with her army at Gloucester on the way to join forces with Lord Pembroke in Wales. Had she succeeded the two armies would have presented a formidable front and the Lancastrian cause might well have triumphed. But Edward IV had pre-empted her move by sending a messenger to Gloucester to command the governor, Sir Richard Beauchamp, to hold out against Margaret until he arrived. Thus the queen found Gloucester's gates closed to her. There was no peaceful haven there for her weary soldiers to rest, nor could they continue the journey to Wales over the River Severn. Instead she headed for Tewkesbury. Edward IV and his brothers, marching along the edge of the Cotswolds, overtook the queen and her son Edward, Prince of Wales and defeated them at Tewkesbury (4 May 1471). The Prince of Wales was killed in the battle and afterwards buried at Tewkesbury Abbey.

Just seven years later George, Duke of Clarence was put

to death for his treason by drowning in a butt of malmsey wine and then buried in Tewkesbury Abbey alongside his duchess, and not far from his previous adversary Edward.

When George's younger brother Richard came to the throne it was the first time a Duke of Gloucester had been king. During a progress in August 1483, Richard III gave Gloucester its famous charter, the quincentenary of which was celebrated in 1983. By the charter Gloucester enjoyed the status of a county and its jurisdiction was extended to cover the hundreds of Dudston and King's Barton, an area of some 45 square miles.

Richard caused much of the building at Sudeley Castle, near Winchcombe, but as far as is known he rarely if ever stayed there after becoming king. Centuries beforehand, the Sudeley estate had been the property of King Ethelred ('the Unready') and then of his daughter Goda, sister of Edward the Confessor. It eventually came to Edward IV and then Richard. After the latter's death at Bosworth in 1485, the castle was given by Henry VII to his uncle the Earl of Pembroke and Duke of Bedford, although when the latter died it reverted to the king's ownership. When Richard's great-nephew succeeded to the throne as Henry VIII in 1509, Sudeley thus became his as Crown property.

Henry VIII spent his honeymoon with Anne Boleyn in Gloucestershire at Painswick and Miserden and it is believed that the pair visited the castle in 1532. Apart from this, though, Henry seemed not to care much for Sudeley and when he died the young Edward VI granted it to his uncle Sir Thomas Seymour, brother of Jane, Henry's third wife. Within weeks of Henry's death, Thomas had married Katherine Parr, the queen dowager, and they both went to

live at Sudeley, accompanied by Lady Jane Grey (whom Katherine wanted to marry Edward VI).

During their short period of happiness at the castle, Katherine and Baron Seymour of Sudeley were visited by Princess Elizabeth (Henry's daughter by Anne Boleyn). It was here that the ragging and romping between the princess and Thomas Seymour was alleged to have taken place.

When Katherine died in 1548, shortly after giving birth to her daughter Mary, she was buried in the castle chapel. Many relics from her life at Sudeley still exist, including her prayer book, which contains an inscription written by Henry VIII.

Elizabeth was again a visitor to Gloucestershire when queen during her royal progresses. The last of her visits was in 1593, when her hosts are recorded as having provided magnificent feasts and entertainment. But the great period of Sudeley's royal patronage was coming to a close and it was later slighted for having taken the wrong side in the Civil War.

With Elizabeth being the last of the Tudors, the succession fell to James VI of Scotland, son of Elizabeth's executed second cousin Mary, Queen of Scots.

James's son Charles I was rapidly embroiled in the Civil War. Gloucestershire played a significant part in the turmoil, and the resistance which Gloucester gave to the royal forces has even been cited as the turning point in the war. Just as Margaret of Anjou had found the city gates closed to her in 1471, so in 1643 Charles found the gates closed and the inhabitants of Gloucester in support of Parliament. His forces laid siege to the city while Charles stayed at Painswick and Matson House. There is a tradition that he also named nearby Paradise at this time: passing through the area early in the war he was struck by its beauty and

Sudeley Castle has had a succession of royal owners including Henry VIII whose third wife, Katherine Parr, came to live here after his death

tranquillity, no doubt in marked contrast to the battle scenes he had to endure, and discovering that it had no particular name he said it was to be called Paradise – as it still is today.

After several months, the siege of Gloucester was raised by Parliamentary reinforcements from London and Charles retired towards Worcester. Some argue that this delay outside Gloucester tipped the balance of the Civil War against Charles. In any case, during the Restoration Charles II ordered the destruction of the city walls as retribution for Gloucester's defiance of his father. Further punishment followed when an Act of Parliament of 1662 took away Gloucester's control of the hundreds of Dudston and King's Barton. Gloucester was thus shrunk to just 317 acres.

Over a century later, recognition and prosperity was brought to the new spa of Cheltenham by the arrival of George III and Queen Charlotte, with three of their daughters, to take the waters. While in the county they were entertained by Lord Ducie and one of the relations of the family at Highgrove, Sir George Onesiphorus Paul. The king mounted expeditions to Gloucester, Tewkesbury, Stroud and Cirencester and during a sightseeing trip to Sudeley Castle he is said to have tumbled down one of the ramshackle staircases. Luckily he was saved by the house-keeper, Mrs Cox, and in gratitude he bestowed a commission in the Guards on one of her relations.

But his visit was not just remembered for its grandiose pursuits. George III also enjoyed talking to local people, including conversing with farmers about animal and land prices. Such could only further his reputation as 'Farmer George', the nickname he had been given for once mentioning fat stock prices during a speech from the throne. He is also reported to have shared a modest repast of mutton and batter pudding with a family in Brockhampton.

In the twentieth century, royal connections with Gloucestershire have been many. Queen Mary, for example, stayed at Badminton for some six years during the Second World War. Princess Alice, Countess of Athlone frequently came to stay at Estcourt Grange, near Highgrove, and for a while Lady Eleanor, a niece of Queen Mary, lived at the Grange. The Duke of Windsor, the future Edward VIII, in the 1920s and '30s stayed from time to time at Easton Grey where he had a hunting box, and he was often to be seen in and around Tetbury.

When three members of the royal family chose in close succession to make their homes in the beautiful southern Cotswolds, close to Cirencester Park and that favourite annual retreat Badminton, it could have been considered a strange coincidence. But history shows that Gloucestershire has always attracted royal interest — and the likelihood is that it will continue to do so.

Highgrove

Highgrove House at Doughton, in the parish of Tetbury, became the home of the Prince and Princess of Wales after their marriage in 1981.

Doughton is a small village (its name probably derives from the Old English *duce*, duck and *tun*, farmstead) which few people outside its immediate locality would have heard of before the arrival of Prince Charles and Princess Diana attracted so much public attention.

The nearby town of Tetbury, on the other hand, seems to have had an eventful past. Flint arrowheads discovered on the site of the present town suggest it was once an early British military station and later, after the Emperor Claudius invaded Britain in AD 43, the Romans occupied the area. Cirencester, several miles away, became a major Roman military base and the second largest town in Roman Britain after London.

The actual name of Tetbury (Old English *Tettanminster*) is thought to derive from a nun called Tetta. In the seventh century, Ethelred of Mercia gave land to Aldhelm, Abbot of Malmesbury, and in AD 680 a religious house was built on it, the founder being Tetta. In the Middle Ages Tetbury

Highgrove House now has a striking architectural elegance. Recent alterations have transformed its appearance (as can be seen by a comparison with the picture on page 6)

thrived as a market town, both during the heyday of the Cotswold wool trade and subsequently as a centre for buying and selling dairy products and meat. There are weekly cattle markets and stall markets held in the town to this day.

Highgrove was built for John Paul Paul by an unknown architect between 1796 and 1798, on an estate which had belonged to his maternal grandfather, Robert Clark.

In *Delineations of Gloucestershire* (1825–7) it was described by J.N. Brewer as:

> a substantial and spacious family residence. The design is entirely free from ostentation, although some ornamental particulars are introduced. The principal efforts of the architect have been directed towards the interior, which presents many good apartments, of accurate proportions, well suited to the domestic and hospitable purposes of a family of high respectability. The situation is fine, and excellent views are obtained from the house and various parts of the attached grounds.

Highgrove was severely damaged by fire in 1893 and nearly £6,000 was spent on its restoration in the following year. In 'The Buildings of England' series, *Gloucestershire, Vol. I. The Cotswolds*, published in 1970, it was described as follows:

> It is a rectangular three-storey block of five by three bays, with pilasters through the upper floors, cornice, and parapet. A nineteenth-century domestic wing was demolished in 1966 and eighteenth-century fireplaces have been introduced into the house from elsewhere.
>
> The garden side has bay windows presumably dating

The original lodge at Highgrove has a fine Venetian window dating to 1798

The wrought-iron gates at the entrance to Highgrove were Tetbury's wedding present to the Prince and Princess

from after 1893. Now a large cedar stands near the house and an attractive garden path is lined with golden yews.

There is a spacious entrance hall with well proportioned reception rooms either side.

The lodge of 1798 survives, with a Venetian window, and rusticated gatepiers with fluted friezes. To this has been added a pair of wrought-iron gates, given to the Prince as a wedding present by the town of Tetbury.

An earlier visual record of Highgrove is provided by *Delineations of Gloucestershire*, which is sometimes called 'Storer's Views' because of the excellent engravings of country houses by J. and H.S. Storer from their own original drawings. They included the lesser country houses, and no

(Over) Even in the early nineteenth century Highgrove was considered 'a substantial and spacious family residence . . . well suited to the domestic and hospitable purposes of a family of high respectability'

Storer's view of Highgrove
conveys an atmosphere of
dignified family life

one could pretend that Highgrove was ever in the top flight
of country houses in the county; but Brewer, who wrote the
text for the Storers, does call it 'this handsome residence',
and the engraving is full of charm. In the engraving the front
elevation of five bays has a central projecting portico with
free-standing columns and a Venetian window above on the
first floor. The central three bays break forward, with
pilasters through the two upper storeys. The roof is low-
pitched behind the cornice and parapet. A carriage and pair
are approaching the house along the drive on the left, and in
the foreground a gentleman on horseback is talking to a lady

and gentleman and a boy with a dog. There is another boy with a dog under a cedar tree, and another gentleman is riding near the house. The park is distinctly flat. Who were these people? The Pauls, observed in the privacy of their home?

The Pauls first came to England as Huguenot immigrants and became established in Gloucestershire in the seventeenth century. They settled in the clothing localities of Woodchester, King's Stanley and Tetbury and, as Dr E.A.L. Moir writes in *Gloucestershire Studies*, they were small, moderately prosperous clothiers, distinguished only by their use of the Biblical Christian names Nathaniel, Onesiphorus, Josiah and Obadiah.

The first Paul to settle in Tetbury was Josiah (d. 1744), son of Nathaniel Paul of King's Stanley. He was succeeded by his son John, who died without issue in 1787 and who was succeeded by his nephew Josiah Paul Tippetts, son of his sister Hester, by her marriage with Richard Tippetts of Dursley. In accordance with the will of his maternal uncle, Josiah Paul Tippetts assumed the name of Paul having married in 1771 Mary, daughter of Robert Clark of Tetbury. Their son John Paul Paul (1772–1828) married Mary, only child of Walter Matthews of Clapham, Surrey in 1793.

John Paul Paul became a notable figure in the community. In 1807, for example, he was High Sheriff of Wiltshire (he had lived at Ashton Keynes, which is in that county). His marriage to Mary Matthews, who was an heiress, put him in the position of being able to build a new house on the estate he had inherited through his mother. This was situated in the hamlet of Doughton, and in 1818 Paul purchased the adjoining manor of Doughton for £25,000 from Thomas Talboys. The latter, so the story goes,

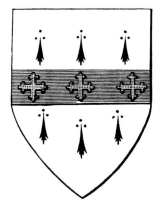

The arms of the Pauls who came to England as Huguenot immigrants in the seventeenth century and settled in Gloucestershire. John Paul Paul (*below*) built Highgrove on the estate which he inherited through his mother

A nineteenth-century drawing of Highgrove shows a much smaller cedar tree and only a one-storey bay window

had lost so much money at the gambling table that he was forced to sell off the family home in order to pay his debts.

When John Paul Paul died in 1828 Highgrove was inherited by his son Walter Matthews Paul, a magistrate for Gloucestershire and Wiltshire, and Captain of the Tetbury troop of the Royal Gloucestershire Yeomanry.

Through successive generations, the Pauls were an influential family in Tetbury and the surrounding area in the nineteenth century. Robert Clark Paul (1775–1856), for example, John Paul Paul's younger brother, had many interests besides that of clothier. He was for a short time in 1801 a partner in Dyehouse Mill on the Nailsworth stream which forms the boundary between Minchinhampton and

Today trees remain an important feature of the estate while Dr Miriam Rothschild has inspired Prince Charles to naturalize bulbs and promote wild flowers in the meadow areas

Woodchester. In 1805 he bought Nag's Head Mill, Cherington, on the Avening stream and his descendants played a leading role in Tetbury as solicitors.

There are several memorials in Tetbury Church to members of the Paul family, including one to Commander Alfred John Paul, RN (1811–45), sixth son of Robert Clark Paul, who entered the Royal Navy in 1824, was a midshipman on HMS *Dartmouth* and flag lieutenant on HMS *Wellesley* at the taking of Chusan and in the operations against Canton and the subsequent capture of the city in 1841. Another memorial is to Josiah Paul, lieutenant in the 69th Regiment of Foot, who died in the service of his country at the Helder on the coast of Holland on 28 September 1799 aged twenty years.

Several members of the Paul family made their careers in the legal field. The *Victoria County History for Gloucestershire*, volume XI, says that the family interest in law apparently originated with John Paul (d. 1787), who was the son of Josiah, the first Paul to settle in Tetbury, and who wrote popular legal manuals. Through the descendants of his great-nephew Robert Clark Paul the family firm prospered. The principal members of the firm, who held in succession the posts of town clerk and clerk to the feoffees, were J.T. Paul (d. 1875), his son A.H. Paul (d. 1900) and his grandson A.P. Kitcat, who sold the practice in 1935.

There can, of course, be drawbacks to one family wielding a large amount of influence in a community. Any number of tales throughout history illustrate the corruption to which a concentration of power in too few (and related) hands can lead. Some of the Pauls, it seems, were not immune to such corruption and recent research by Ted Prince of the History of Tetbury Society has uncovered a rather involved, but

Highgrove has always had strong ties with the town of Tetbury, many of the Pauls holding official posts in the town throughout the nineteenth and early twentieth centuries

nonetheless fascinating saga. It makes interesting reading and brings colour and life to the historical record of the Paul family.

Mr Prince was first alerted to something untoward having taken place during the Paul era when he was researching the records of the local feoffees. Their minutes from 1824–8 were missing, and it seemed this could be no mere accident. Indeed, he had come upon a scandal which involved both John Paul Paul, who had Highgrove built, and his brother Robert Clark Paul.

The feoffees originated in 1633, when the lordship of the manor of Tetbury was bought from the Berkeleys by the townspeople. From then on, two bodies of people, The Feoffees and The Thirteen, had the responsibility of managing the manor. Details of the exact authority of the feoffees are somewhat complicated, but broadly it can be said that they virtually ran the town until they lost most of their considerable (even if rather ill-defined) powers through the various Acts of Parliament that brought about 'modern' local government by stages in the nineteenth century.

The interest of this particular story is in their capacity as trustees of the Tetbury Charity and its management of the charitable estates, local rents and tolls – and an accusation that they were diverting funds from their proper use.

John Paul Paul was one of the trustees during the 1820s, as was his brother Robert Clark Paul. It happened also that John Letall, Robert Clark's partner in the law firm of Letall and Paul, was clerk to the feoffees and trustees as well as town clerk. So, between them, the three men held a good deal of power and in fact the other trustees seem to have been quite happy to leave the management of the charitable estates entirely to Letall and his partner Robert Clark Paul

The Reverend Samuel Paul Paul is commemorated in Tetbury Church, but his appointment, given the unscrupulous way it came about, left much bad feeling in the town

(which does not say much for their own sense of responsibility).

In 1824 John Stone, a newcomer to the town, made public a carefully worded accusation that John Letall and Robert Clark Paul had effectively taken over complete control of the Charity estates and that instead of using funds for charitable purposes they were lining their own pockets and spending the money on their own entertainment. In the absence of proper accounts – which should have been published every year – concrete evidence was difficult to produce to prove the claim. However, Stone could point to one striking instance of a misapplication of money: The Court Dinner, or 'The Lords' Guttling Day' as it was popularly known. This was an extravagant feasting and drinking event which alone swallowed up almost enough money to have funded the posts of schoolmaster and lecturer – two situations which for many years had not been filled because, it was said, the profits deriving from tolls and markets which were intended to maintain them had been insufficient.

Other examples of misappropriated money were cited, and, for good measure, Stone had launched a second line of attack on the Paul family, which involved the appointment of the vicar of Tetbury – an appointment which, it just so happened, was made by the trustees. The Advowson (right to appoint the vicar) was of great value, Stone argued, as the vicarage would provide its incumbent with a comfortable income for life. John Paul Paul and Robert Clark Paul had persuaded the feoffees to give the position of vicar to their brother Samuel, who had been an officer in the Gloucestershire Militia, but who had left the army for this new prospect. The whole situation, Stone implied, smacked of

unfair preference of a relative and, in any case, he maintained that the living should not be given away, but sold and the money used to benefit the town. It was also, of course, in extreme bad taste to be arranging the appointment of a new vicar when the existing one, 77-year-old Richard Davies, was still alive.

There seems no doubt that the Pauls were guilty of the two accusations. Indeed, during an argument with a certain Mr Biedermann, Robert Clark Paul had openly admitted both that it was his intention to wrest total control of the Charity estates into his family's hands and that the living which Samuel was on the verge of being given would thereafter remain in the family.

The case was heard before Vice-Chancellor Leach in December 1824. Needless to say, John Letall and Robert Clark Paul did their best to obfuscate matters – one suspects their legal minds stood them in good stead – and the consequent verdict amounted to little more than a judicial slap on the wrists for the feoffees. The wastage of money, for example on 'The Lords' Guttling Day', was, however, heavily criticised and the Vice-Chancellor directed that the court should prescribe rules to avoid any further 'misapplication and excess of authority'. As for the matter of Samuel Paul Paul: the court does not appear to have followed up its demand for an explanation from the feoffees of their behaviour with regard to his appointment as vicar and the feoffees went ahead with it regardless. Leach, it should be noted, was a man notorious for his deficiencies as a vice-chancellor, and this could well explain why the feoffees were not severely called to account. A plaque in St Mary's records that Samuel Paul Paul was vicar from 1825–8.

Apart from this turbulent episode, members of the Paul

The back of the house provides a secluded patch of garden shaded by a giant cedar tree

family can be recalled for more illustrious reasons, as already mentioned. Indeed, a descendant of Robert Clark Paul himself is remembered particularly for his sporting prowess. This was Sidney Austyn Paul Kitcat, born at Tetbury in 1868, the son of Clara Frances Paul (Robert Clark's daughter) and the Revd David Kitcat, rector of Lasborough from 1859 to 1906, who lived at Tetbury.

Sidney Austyn Paul Kitcat has some claim to fame, for not only was he captain of the Marlborough College cricket XI in 1886, making 204 not out against the Old Marlburians, but he caused the MCC to make an alteration in the laws of cricket. When batting for Marlborough against Rugby he was given out after being caught at cover-point off the bowling of C.W. Bengough, who through an oversight was bowling at the wrong end. The matter was referred to the MCC, the law then stating that 'the bowler may not change ends more than twice in the innings, nor bowl more than two overs in succession'. The law was amended in 1889, allowing a bowler 'to change ends as often as he pleases, provided that he does not bowl two consecutive overs in one innings'.

At the early age of thirteen, Kitcat played for Gloucestershire Colts against Gloucestershire in April 1882, but was not tried for the county until 1891. Among his best scores for Gloucestershire were 95 not out against Middlesex at Lord's in 1897, which secured him a place in the Gentlemen's side against the Players at the Oval that summer, and 77 not out against Sussex at Bristol in 1896, when he and W.G. Grace (301) added 193 for the ninth wicket, which is still the Gloucestershire record for that wicket.

But, to return to Walter Matthews Paul, the owner of Highgrove (1828–60). His sister Mary married her kinsman

Gloucestershire cricketer, S.A.P. Kitcat (cousin of the Pauls of Highgrove), and W.G. Grace (*below*) together added 193 for the ninth wicket against Sussex in 1896 – one of the great Gloucestershire records

Sir George Onesiphorus Paul
who became the famous
prison reformer. In his
younger days he had kept a
stable of about a dozen
racehorses. His memorial is
in Gloucester Cathedral

Sir John Dean Paul, Bart. in 1835. Sir John Dean Paul was descended from the Revd Nicholas Paul of Berkeley (d. 1650), who was the father of Nicholas and the Revd Onesiphorus Paul of Wanborough, Wilts. Nicholas II married Elizabeth, daughter of Thomas Dean of Woodchester and she inherited Southfields Mill, Woodchester, where Frederick, Prince of Wales was later entertained. Dean Paul (d. 1794) and Sir Onesiphorus Paul, first baronet, were their sons. The latter's son, Sir George Onesiphorus Paul, second baronet, after an extravagant life in which he kept a stable of about a dozen horses and was a regular supporter of all the local races at Tetbury, Cirencester, Monmouth and Bath, became the famous prison reformer, whose memorial is to be found in Gloucester Cathedral.

When Sir George died in 1820 the baronetcy became extinct, but it was revived in 1821 when Dean Paul's grandson John Dean became the first of the new creation. The latter's first wife was the granddaughter of the eighth Earl of Strathmore, from whom the Queen Mother is descended, and therefore also Prince Charles, current resident of Highgrove. Sir John Dean Paul was the son of John Dean Paul of Salisbury, who married Frances, daughter of Robert Snow of the firm of Snow, Paul and Co., bankers in London.

Walter Matthews Paul's sister Mary, therefore, was the stepmother of the second baronet, Sir John Dean Paul (1802–68), a banker who, to quote the *Dictionary of National Biography*, belonged to the firm of William Strahan, Paul and Robert Makin Bates, which suspended payment in 1855, for which the partners were severally sentenced to fourteen years' penal servitude, as they had fraudulently disposed of their clients' securities.

Sir John was transported to Australia and later the *Madras Times* gave some 'curious information' respecting the 'notorious fraudulent banker, Sir John Dean Paul, Bart., late of Rodborough Manor'. Immediately after he was sentenced to penal servitude, the report stated, Lady Paul realized all the property settled upon her, and proceeded without delay to Sydney, where she purchased a beautiful seat in the suburbs. Her husband having arrived at a penal settlement in another part of Australia, as one of a gang of convicts, she applied to the Government for his services, and was permit-

The annual Tetbury mop survived despite attempts to ban it by William Hamilton Yatman who took over Highgrove in the 1860s

ted to employ him as her 'assigned servant'. The report added that having thus released him from unpleasant restraint, she placed all the newly-purchased property in his hands, and she had since led a quiet life in his company.

In 1860 Walter Matthews Paul sold the combined estate of Doughton Manor and Highgrove to Colonel E.J. Strachey and it was acquired three to four years later by William Hamilton Yatman, a barrister.

Yatman came to Highgrove from Wellesbourne Manor, near Warwick. He was soon a prominent figure among the feoffees at Tetbury, although he seems not infrequently to have been absent from Highgrove, attending to property interests he had in Bournemouth. Nevertheless, he is remembered at Tetbury as a great benefactor and contributor to the community.

One of the local incidents in which Yatman was involved should raise wry smiles even today since it relates to an issue which periodically crops up for debate in Tetbury: he sought to ban the annual mop, something which certain people have in subsequent years also tried to do.

The mop was established in 1802 as a hiring fair at which servants and labourers could literally parade themselves for selection by masters. Of course, when it was first begun, the mop served a very good purpose in bringing together those seeking work and those seeking workers. There had been, after all, less means of self-advertisement through post and newspapers (if the servants could read and write) than in Yatman's time. But, nearly eighty years on some people were of the opinion that the mop had outlived its original purpose and that it was moreover rather degrading to those employees who put their services up for 'sale'. By this time, too, the mop had deteriorated somewhat into a great day for drinking and general debauchery, which the police were simply resigned to letting happen and which led to many subsequent days of lost work while the revellers recovered from their excesses. This state of affairs gave Yatman further fuel for his argument for a ban.

So it was that in 1878 he wrote to the feoffees (his letter was addressed to A. Paul, clerk of the feoffees and descendant of the Pauls of Highgrove) to protest about the event. He himself was absent from the feoffee meeting at which the complaint was considered and it appears that after discussion, the matter was simply dropped, not, apparently, to be raised again by Yatman. No doubt the feoffees realized the magnitude of the ill-feeling which moves to ban the mop would create and chose, like the police, to turn a blind eye!

Despite attempts from time to time since to stop the mop it continues to this day, although its function as a hiring fair ceased many years ago. Today it is a small annual fun-fair which bears no resemblance to its origins.

Most of all, Yatman is to be remembered for his benevolence

Yatman financed the rebuilding of Tetbury tower and spire. The tower was split to the foundations and the spire was leaning to one side. Today, Prince Charles is patron of a new fund-raising appeal

Tetbury Church can still be seen from the front door of Highgrove. Yatman maintained the gap in the trees to ensure that he could see the spire

and generosity, including the giving of financial assistance to schools and a hospital. He also brought life to the local community through helping to found the Tetbury cattle market in 1890, which celebrated its centenary in 1990 with a special cattle auction. Annually, it now has a turnover approaching £2 million.

Yatman's greatest lasting benefaction was a gift of much-needed money for repairs to St Mary's, Tetbury's parish church. Like the mop, this is a current issue still, as St Mary's is again facing repairs, and once again it is notable that an inhabitant of Highgrove, Prince Charles, is very much involved in the project as patron of the fund-raising appeal.

The original church on the site of St Mary's was probably built sometime after 1400, but this had been pulled down, except for the tower and spire, in 1777, and rebuilt under the superintendence of Francis Hiorne of Warwick, at a cost of some £5,000. By 1890, the tower and spire were in a

decision to retire but mature consideration confirms my previous view that it is not right for an absentee (I am too old to rebuild and must therefore though reluctantly sell Highgrove) to undertake duties which he cannot personally enter upon and constantly go through with

dangerous condition – the tower was split from the parapet to the foundation and the spire was reported to lean 4 foot 6 inches to the south and 8 inches to the east – so they were taken down and rebuilt in replica. Yatman financed the project, which cost in the region of £10,000. He undertook this largely as a tribute to the memory of his beloved son, William, a captain in the Dragoon Guards. As a young man at Highgrove, William had worshipped at St Mary's, but his life was sadly cut short when he died in 1884 from a lung abscess, aged just thirty-one. The depth of his father's affection was further marked by the clearance of an avenue leading from the front of the house at Highgrove – so that Yatman could see the church spire from the windows of his home.

There is a poignant aspect to this story, because even before the repairs to the church had been completed, the bells were set ringing to summon the fire brigade to attend to the fire of 1893 at Highgrove. S.G. Mosdell, who has researched the life story of Yatman, gave a graphic account of the events in an article published in *Gloucestershire and Avon Life* (September 1984). In the early hours of the morning, the horse-drawn brigade rushed to the scene. Neighbours in Doughton had already helped to retrieve some furnishings, but the fire had a good hold. When the light dawned the

(*Below*) The memorial in Tetbury Church to Yatman's much-loved son William. His tragic death was followed by a disastrous fire at Highgrove which forced Yatman to sell up and resign office as a feoffee (*above*)

Highgrove as it looked when it was sold to the Duchy of Cornwall by Maurice Macmillan in 1980

next day, it revealed the main block and the back of the house severely damaged. Luckily Yatman and his wife Elizabeth had been away in Bournemouth on the night of the disaster and the staff at Highgrove all escaped unscathed. But the episode brought about Yatman's departure from the estate: it is thought that he was under-insured and rather than face the huge repairs needed he decided to sell Highgrove. He and his wife went to live in Bournemouth. The couple did return to celebrate the completion of work at St Mary's, but the occasion must have been a mixture of great sadness with any joy.

The Highgrove estate was acquired by Arthur Charles Mitchell (1847–1917) and he immediately set to the work of rebuilding the wrecked house. He used the architect John Hart, of Bristol, and repairs cost almost £6,000. This, Mr Mosdell records, included the provision of an improved drainage system, a luggage lift to bedrooms on the first and second floors, and an engine to pump water and later to supply electricity. The interior walls were built on metal frames, there was a teak entrance floor and staircase, and an inglenook-shaped dining room. Outside, tennis courts were established in the gardens and the drive was resurfaced.

Arthur Charles Mitchell was married first to Laura Harriet (d. 1874), daughter of Sir Michael Hicks-Beach, eighth baronet, and secondly to Constance Lucy (d. 1945), daughter of John Elwes of Colesborne. When he died, A.C. Mitchell was succeeded by his son Lieutenant-Colonel Francis Arthur Mitchell (1888–1955), who commanded the Royal Gloucestershire Hussars. Francis Arthur, though, lived at Doughton Manor while his mother Constance continued to reside at Highgrove.

Constance Mitchell was crippled for many years with arthritis and when she appeared in Tetbury, it was in a large chauffeur-driven car which could accommodate her wheelchair. She had many servants at her beck and call and she is remembered as very Victorian in her manner, always dressed in black skirts down to the ground, perhaps a rather distant figure. Yet she was a kindly lady, too, as an incident remembered by old Tetburian Fred Cook illustrates.

Fred was an errand boy for Mac Fisheries in Tetbury before the First World War, serving both Highgrove and Gatcombe Park. It was, of course, customary for all deliveries to be made at the side entrance at Highgrove. One day, encountering Mrs Mitchell, Fred politely remarked upon the beauty of Highgrove, at which she urged him to come to look at the view from the front – a gesture which was, so Fred reminisces, quite out of order, considering his position. They discussed the exquisite view of St Mary's Church and the tale of Yatman – and from that day on, Mrs Mitchell insisted that Fred should cycle up the front drive with his deliveries and not bother with the side entrance. He prized the privilege.

Fred did not enjoy quite such luck when he cycled to Gatcombe, which at that time was owned by the Ricardo family. Although the setting of the house was spectacular, the hill he had to climb up towards it was always tiresome. Understandably, he was not too upset when the Ricardos decided one day, without giving any particular reason, to transfer their custom to a fishmonger elsewhere!

By the 1950s, Lieutenant-Colonel Gwyn and the Hon. Mrs Morgan-Jones were living at Highgrove. They were popular figures, not least because each year they allowed the Beaufort Pony Club, to which their own children belonged, to use the estate grounds for its instruction week. It was always a grand affair, with competitions over jumps and courses, and a special award for the best student of the week.

The atmosphere at Highgrove seems to have been more relaxed under the Morgan-Joneses, in many ways a sign of the times. Servants recall being treated almost like members of the family, although they still observed their proper place and if they forgot would be gently reminded. For one former servant, this meant being reprimanded for wearing perfume when she served dinner. The reason for the rebuke? She might have masked the perfume of the guests!

In 1965 it was time for change again. Highgrove was purchased by the Macmillan family trust for a reported

£89,000 and it became home to Maurice Macmillan, Conservative MP for Farnham, son of Harold Macmillan, Prime Minister 1957–63.

For at least some of the time of Macmillan's ownership, Highgrove was let out. Peter Harding, of Tetbury, recalls that Elliott Roosevelt, the son of President Franklin D. Roosevelt, stayed there for two years. He told Mr Harding that he was doing some writing and that he enjoyed Highgrove for the peace and quiet it gave him and his wife.

When he did live at Highgrove, Maurice Macmillan was well-liked by those who worked for him. His father Harold was not an uncommon sight in Tetbury, often stopping to chat to people.

During their ownership, the Macmillans removed one wing of Highgrove House, to make it more easily manageable as a family home. Apart from this, no major alterations were carried out. In its advertisement for sale in 1980 (Maurice, suffering from ill health, had given up his Cotswold hunting activities, and intended to live with his father at Birch Grove in Sussex), Highgrove was described as: 'A distinguished Georgian house standing in superb parkland in the Duke of Beaufort's Hunt. Entrance hall, four principal reception rooms, domestic quarters, nine bedrooms, six bathrooms, nursery wing. Full central heating. Fine stable block. Easily managed gardens. Lodge. Farm manager's house. Pair of farm cottages. Dairy unit and farm buildings. In all about 347 acres.' In short: it was a residence fit for a prince.

The Duchy of Cornwall purchased Highgrove for a sum in the region of £750,000–£1 million. It was an ideal setting: Prince Charles could ride with the Beaufort Hunt and play polo at Cirencester, and there was an estate to farm and develop.

The Prince of Wales in his own special hunting livery

(Over) Three spouting whales provide a fountain centrepiece to the stone terrace at the back of the house

47

Before Prince Charles and Princess Diana moved in, considerable renovation needed to be done, including major work on the inside of the house. The interior designer the royal couple chose was Dudley Poplak.

To welcome the new inhabitants of Highgrove, the local people of Doughton presented them with a wedding gift of a weather vane, to be placed on top of Highgrove stables. It was made by John Craston at his forge in Brightwell-cum-Satwell, near Wallingford, Oxfordshire, and formed the silhouette of a horse-drawn plough and ploughman.

The people of Tetbury, too, gave their gift: wrought-iron gates for the driveway, made by local craftsman Hector Cole.

Highgrove House itself has undergone considerable external changes over the last ten years, all closely supervised by Prince Charles, as might be expected from his keen interest in architecture. The creeper, which had gradually spread over the exterior, was cleared and the stone was cleaned to restore it to its translucent splendour. Then came more exciting and imaginative developments, the ideas for which were inspired by a painting by the artist Felix Kelly.

Mr Kelly created a picture of Highgrove House as it *might* look, approached from the drive. The ideas expressed in the painting were converted to technical drawings and realized by architect Peter Falconer, from Stroud. The solid stone parapet with balls along the top of the house, which was rather austere in appearance, was taken down and replaced by balustrading made of Bath stone, and more elegant urns replaced the balls. The front entrance was enhanced by removing the existing pilasters and replacing them with new ones with Ionic capitals and a pediment with a roundel

Prince Charles's keen interest in architecture shows in the imaginative changes to Highgrove's façade

window. Where possible, the stone removed from the old parapet was used for the pediment. In the porch itself glazing bars were added over the door. The effect of these alterations was to lift the whole aspect of the house, transforming it from a rather solid block to an altogether more ornate and elegant building.

The most recent development has been the completion of a small single-storey extension to the house, carried out by architect William Bertram, of Bath. This extension is on the site of the old wing demolished in 1966, although it is not quite so large. The old wing contained pantries, a scullery and a coalhouse, but the new construction provides a reception room for the many official visitors and an office for Prince Charles's Private Secretary. The design is adventurous, being quite different from the rest of the house: built of Cotswold walling stone with Bath stone detailing and a slate roof, it has a cottage-like appearance which offers a more informal welcome to visitors than the main house.

Other work undertaken outside includes the enlargement of the gravel drive in front of the house and the installation of a swimming pool. Lots of smaller details have been added, too, like a ridge-tile dovecote, which was presented to Prince Charles and Princess Diana by the Sultan of Oman, and is approached from the house by an avenue of lime. Benches, designed by Mr Bertram, now give the opportunity to sit comfortably beneath some of the trees (and there has been extensive planting of trees throughout the estate).

Further afield, on Street Farm on the edge of the estate, old farm buildings have been converted, through a Duchy of Cornwall scheme backed by CoSIRA (now the Rural Development Commission), to create five light industrial/

The Sultan of Oman presented the royal couple with an ornate ridge-tile dovecote (*above*) and Prince Charles himself commissioned David Wynne to provide the sculpture for the secret woodland garden (*below*) with its children's tree house

craft workshops. Street Farm was purchased from Maurice Macmillan shortly after Highgrove and represents a leading example of the good use to which derelict rural buildings can be put.

Although not on the Highgrove estate, the restoration work being carried out at St Mary's, Tetbury's parish church, should be mentioned, since it offers an interesting link to the rebuilding of a century ago, which was so generously funded by William Hamilton Yatman, owner of Highgrove. By 1990 the church was badly in need of repair. The roof and stonework was deteriorating, there had been flood damage from winter rains penetrating the nave windows, the electrical and heating systems needed urgent attention. Work estimated to cost £500,000 would have to be carried out. A restoration and improvement fund was set up in October 1990 and Prince Charles became patron of the appeal. His financial and moral support and his support through hosting an evening reception at Highgrove to aid the fund-raising have in many ways reaffirmed the Highgrove–St Mary's link established by Yatman. The church, with its spire still visible from Highgrove to this day, has already had some £90,000 of work carried out on its exterior and work on the interior is now under way.

The second great change at Highgrove besides the architectural alterations and additions is the development of the farming of the estate. When the Duchy of Cornwall originally acquired the estate, it extended to some 347 acres. Further acquisitions of land, such as Broadfield Farm, Tetbury, and Happylands, on the edge of Highgrove, have increased the acreage of farmland to approximately 1,050 acres. Close to Highgrove House new farm buildings have been built: the old dairy has been pulled down and a new

Farm buildings have been given as much attention at Highgrove as house and garden, using a combination of modern techniques and sympathetic building materials

steel-framed building clad with stone and with a stone-tiled roof has been erected for the Aberdeen Angus on the estate. Other farm buildings are to be constructed to replace the old Dutch barn. Also in the farm building area, it is interesting to note a recently completed acquatic plant sewage treatment system which, while being an environmentally friendly method of treating sewage, also creates an attractive feature of an area of reeds, willow and an ornamental pond which blends in naturally with the general farm buildings.

Farming interest at the home farms centres on the dairy herd, sheep, beef cows and crops such as wheat, barley, rape and beans. Produce is supplied to the normal national outlets, such as the Milk Marketing Board, although a certain amount goes direct to local people. One such

David Chubb makes bee
skeps out of straw from the
Highgrove estate

example is David Chubb, of South Cerney, who makes bee
skeps. Some of the straw he uses is purchased from Highgrove.

Prince Charles's aim at Highgrove is to convert all
farming to organic methods. A controlled switch began in
1985 and the target, says farm director Terry Summers, is to
convert the total acreage by 1996. By the end of 1991
approximately 115 acres had been converted. The first Soil
Association certified crop was produced in 1988. The following year, the 40-ton wheat harvest was used to produce
the much-publicized Highgrove stoneground wholemeal
loaf, sold through Tesco. There will be more such Highgrove labels to watch out for, says Mr Summers, once the
organic conversion has been effected.

One feels that Highgrove today is an estate which probably flourishes more than at any other time in the past and
that its full potential as a property is being explored and
realized.

In the woodland garden a
beehive has its own special
thatched shelter

The Garden at Highgrove

BY ROSEMARY VEREY

The Prince of Wales has transformed the avenue of golden yews, replacing the gravel path with a paved thyme walk

In 1980 there was virtually no garden to anchor the house into its setting. An old cedar tree outside the study window and the clipped golden yews flanking the gravel path were the only worthwhile features. Through the Prince of Wales's interest in design and planting, the garden has evolved year by year, and now the house is surrounded by a diversity of elements, each with its own character.

The drive approaches the house on its east side, and there is an immediate feeling of welcome, with interesting planting and stone vases either side of the front door and climbers to set off the beauty of the Cotswold stone. An 8-foot yew hedge on the left continues the line of the house and forms one of the walls enclosing a south-facing garden room filled with old-fashioned roses and edged with box and lavender. Lady Salisbury gave invaluable advice here with the layout and planting. This garden makes a satisfying view from a bow-fronted drawing-room window.

On the west front, on each side of the long gravel path with its eleven pairs of golden yews, a design of pleached hornbeams was laid out with the help of Russell Vernon-Smith, and the Prince of Wales decided that this large area of lawn should be framed by yew hedges. Recently, Sir Roy Strong has given these hedges added impact by clipping them in the shape of swags, and piercing windows through those surrounding the rose garden.

To provide this predominantly green area with further character, the prince has added stone seats set back into the pattern of hedges. Stone statues and huge clay 'Ali Baba' pots in perfect proportion help to enhance and co-ordinate the elements of the composition. The stark gravel path, 90 yards long, always irked the Prince; one of his latest ideas has been to remove the gravel and lay large flat stones (gathered from the estate) down the centre. Hundreds of thyme plants of different varieties now create a fragrant strip on each side – most of them grown from cuttings and planted by the Prince himself.

The main garden door leads down a flight of steps to the stone terrace, where a pond with a Simon Verity fountain of three spouting whales is the central feature. The Prince is keen to improve the planting here – it is a place much used for sitting and entertaining.

Old-fashioned roses surround the sundial on the south side of the house

Statues, a summerhouse and huge clay pots enhance the carefully co-ordinated planting at Highgrove

The cottage garden is full of
variety, with a pleasing sense
of informality

I hope I have left my own mark on the cottage and
woodland gardens. The former, near the house and where
the Princess of Wales likes to sit, was laid out in the spring
of 1988. It was a day of vibrant activity, HRH on his knees
planting with the rest of us, and young Prince William
giving each plant its ration of fertilizer and making sure we
all worked hard. A wooden rose-covered archway leads from
the cottage garden into another section where trees and
shrubs predominate. In the winter of 1991 the Prince
created the outline of more borders, which he is planning to
fill with unusual species, many of them scented.

Several trees in the woodland garden were blown down in
the storm of January 1990, and this provided the opportunity to add ornamental trees and to make a pattern of
mown grass paths around beds of woodland shrubs, spring
bulbs and summer flowering ground cover. It was the

A secluded walled path leads
from the meadowland to the
enclosed vegetable garden

The fountain and herb beds form the centre to Highgrove's magnificent walled potager

prince's inspiration, and he loves this place. He wants it to become an enclosed, secret area and has been busy planning and planting surrounding hedges and windbreaks.

Another important feature especially loved and enjoyed by the Prince is his 0.73 acre walled potager, designed with Lady Salisbury's help. This has developed from strength to strength under the care of Dennis Brown with his skill at vegetable growing, but it was HRH who established the structure of the arbours and the planting of the perimeter beds with fragrant herbs, dianthus and bulbs. A striking feature is the circle of pleached *Malus* 'Golden Hornet' around the central herb beds and fountain.

Perimeter beds and walls are richly planted with herbs, flowers and fruit trees

A shady arbour overlooks the
vegetable garden and offers
an oasis of peace

The great wild flower pioneer in England, Miriam Rothschild, has inspired the Prince to sow wild flower seed along
the verges of his front drive and to naturalize bulbs in his
meadowland on the way to the potager and woodland
garden.

Although the concepts are fundamentally the Prince's,
they are enriched by his advisers' practical experience and
carried out by his two talented and youthful gardeners,
David Magson and James Aldridge. The influence of Paddy
Whiteland, the Irishman who arrived at Highgrove about
forty years ago as head groom, still pervades the estate.

HRH combines an ever-widening knowledge in horticul-
ture with his gift for inspiring others. The garden and its
surrounding estate will continue to develop as a place of real
beauty.

Gatcombe Park

Gatcombe Park became the home of the Princess Royal and Captain Mark Phillips in 1976. It is adjacent to the Avening stream, which marks the boundary between the parishes of Avening and Minchinhampton, although it is actually situated in the latter.

The Minchinhampton–Avening area is rich with the remains of neolithic man. His burying places, or barrows, are to be found on the Gatcombe estate, Minchinhampton Common and the Copse at Avening. At one time it was believed that such tumuli contained buried treasures and a number of them were disturbed by fortune hunters. One local believer in the theory, called Molly Dreamer because of her fantasies, is known to have dug into the Gatcombe Lodge barrow (among others) at the beginning of the nineteenth century. There is certainly no record of her finding anything, but around 1870 a workman employed at Gatcombe did discover a sepulchral chamber within the barrow, which contained a skeleton. It was a valuable find, but not quite in the way Molly might have hoped. Elsewhere, flint implements provide further evidence of early man's existence, and the remnants of pit dwellings show

(Over) The grandeur of Gatcombe lies in its setting, bounded by beech woods and looking out over an idyllic Cotswold landscape

The Long Stone opposite the
entrance to Gatcombe Park.
Superstition held that it had
power to cure rickets

where he lived on the common.

There are also two fine Stone Age monoliths, one of
which, known as the Long Stone, stands on the north side of
the main road within a short distance of Gatcombe Lodge
entrance. Tradition has it that superstitious mothers were
in the habit of passing ricketty children through a hole in
the Long Stone, or 'Holey Stone', with the idea that this
would make them strong again.

Another mysterious site is the so-called Devil's Churchyard to the east, now part of the Gatcombe estate. There is a local tradition that a stone circle once stood here and that the stones were moved to The Lammas, Minchinhampton, because unholy rites had been performed on the site. The story is told that it was intended to build a church here – but the building done during the day was pushed down by the Devil during the night, until eventually a new site was chosen and the church built at Minchinhampton.

For much of their history, the two parishes of Avening and Minchinhampton have been inextricably bound together, being under the single control of successive owners from the Conquest to the early nineteenth century. After the Norman invasion of 1066, both Avening and 'Hampton', as it was then known, were given by William the Conqueror's wife Mathilda to the Convent of the Holy Trinity at Caen. The actual name Minchinhampton can be traced to this act: Minchin derives from the Middle English rendering of the Anglo-Saxon *Mynece, Munechene* the Nuns' Hampton. For some five hundred years, until the Dissolution of the Monasteries, the parishes remained in the possession of the Church.

Both manors were 'granted' to Andrew, first Baron Windsor, by Henry VIII, 'in exchange' for Stanwell, Middlesex in 1543. The Windsor family had lived at Stanwell for many generations, but Henry decided that their residence was too close to his own property of Windsor. He duly invited himself to dinner with Baron Windsor and afterwards made it known that he liked Stanwell so much that he would have it in exchange for some other properties in Worcestershire and Gloucestershire. The baron

A stone marker in the middle of the estate bears witness to a complex history of parish boundaries

An old view of Minchinhampton Church. To the right stands the old manor house, home of the Sheppard family before they built Gatcombe

protested at the 'exchange' but to no avail. Nor did the episode have a happy conclusion, because Baron Windsor died the following year. What time he could have spent at Gatcombe is not known.

Minchinhampton and Avening remained in the Windsor family until 1642, when Thomas, Lord Windsor bequeathed them to his nephew Thomas Hickman. Lord Windsor must have had substantial debts because the trustees of Hickman, who was a minor, were obliged to sell the manors in 1651 to Samuel Sheppard.

The Sheppard family played an important role in the history of Minchinhampton and Avening for some two hundred years. They were wealthy clothiers at a time when the woollen cloth industry in the area prospered, and they were figures of note in the community. Samuel Sheppard

III, for example, was a Justice of the Peace and High Sheriff of Gloucestershire in 1730. It was his son Edward who, on coming into possession of the family property, had a new house built at Gatcombe, which was no doubt thought better to reflect the Sheppards' standing. The manor house at Minchinhampton had been adjacent to the church on the site of the present school, but, being hemmed in by both town and common, its park would probably have been considered inadequate to the dignity which the Sheppards had attained. The new house at Gatcombe, built 1771–4, was in a beautiful situation about a mile from Minchinhampton.

'The elegant modern seat of the Sheppard family', as the historian Thomas Fosbroke described it, was a fine mansion with a very good front elevation. The plaster work inside the house was in the Adam style, and all the details were extremely well carried out.

Francis Franklin of Chalford was the mason responsible and possibly the designer, In *c.* 1820, after the house had been bought by David Ricardo MP, the political economist, wings were added by George Basevi, famous pupil of the classic revivalist architect Sir John Soane and himself the distinguished architect of the Fitzwilliam Museum at Cambridge. A conservatory was built on in 1829, but little after that happened to change the appearance of Gatcombe.

The central block, with two storeys and a basement, is faced in ashlar and crowned with a moulded cornice and balustraded parapet. The centre breaks forward with an open pediment above a Venetian window opening on to a balustraded balcony above the porch which has four Doric columns. Either side are one storey bowed wings. The entrance hall gives on to the main staircase, which is partly

George Basevi, cousin of Benjamin Disraeli, was architect of the bowed wings (*below*) added to Gatcombe around 1820. His bust is in the Fitzwilliam Museum, Cambridge, which he also designed

The broad sweep of
Gatcombe's imposing façade
with its recently restored
conservatory

screened from it by a pair of tall Doric columns. The east
side contains the dining-room, and the library is beyond, in
the single-storeyed wing. The west side has two drawing-
rooms, with the conservatory beyond. The principal rooms
have carved marble chimney-pieces.

The stables are built round a polygonal yard with an
embattled wall facing the buildings. The grounds are splen-
didly landscaped, and very pretty.

Gatcombe was among the properties featured in *Delineations of Gloucestershire* and described by J.N. Brewer.
Gatcombe, he wrote:

is placed on the ascent of a narrow valley, bounded by
high beech wood, with intermingled oak and ash, on one
side, whilst the rising ground, in an opposite direction, is
decorated with clumps and other efforts of the landscape
gardener. The house looks down on a spacious and fine
lawn, which terminates in waters, expanded by the hand
or art to an ornamental breadth of space. The present

elegant house is a well-proportioned and spacious mansion, handsome on the exterior and internally well designed and arranged. The chief portico of entrance is
highly ornamental to the fabric, and the fine and very
extensive conservatory, which adjoins one end of the
house and runs in a line with the principal front, is
chastely planned and delicately executed.

Edward Sheppard, the builder of Gatcombe, who married
Sarah, daughter of Charles Coxe of Kemble House, a family
which had also had connections with Nether Lypiatt Manor,
died in 1803 aged seventy-eight. By this time, his new
property had already been mortgaged, which suggests that
the costs involved in having Gatcombe house built had been
considerable indeed. Edward's only son and heir, Philip
(1766–1838), became the last Sheppard owner of the
estates.

Philip was described by A.T. Playne, in his history of
Avening and Minchinhampton, as having been an easy-

Gatcombe's original stable
block is built round a
polygonal yard

Storer's view of Gatcombe –
'a well-proportioned and
spacious manor'

going, good-natured man, very extravagant, and with a
great taste for sport and expensive amusements. He raised a
troop of Yeomanry in 1795, the equipment and maintenance
of which cost him a lot of money. He also kept a pack of
hounds at Gatcombe, which were not looked upon with
much favour by his father, if we may judge from an entry in
a pocket-book of 1790:

> Phil talked of giving up ye hounds; I hope he may
> continue in ye resolution.

There is, also, in the same pocket-book an account of a great
run which Philip had with his hounds from Calcot Barn.

All this now, of course, is Beaufort country. Sheppard was hunting his hounds when the 5th Duke (Master 1786–1803) was increasingly changing his preference from stag- to fox-hunting.

On his accession to the estate, Philip Sheppard continued his career of extravagance and endeavoured to stave off ruin by mortgages and disposing of parts of his inheritance. Long into the night he and his steward Baldwin would hold consultations to devise ways and means of tiding over the more pressing difficulties; but the crash came in 1812 and Sheppard escaped to Dunkirk in France, out of reach of his creditors. He eventually died in London in 1838 in very reduced circumstances, leaving two sons, Edward and Philip Charles.

Although he had come to a sorry end, Philip seems to have maintained his unrepentantly flamboyant outlook from start to finish. There is a story told by A.T. Playne concerning another extravagant inhabitant of Minchinhampton which illustrates the point well: a certain William Whitehead attained notoriety for recklessly spending his way through some £100,000, which he had inherited from his father. In just thirteen months around 1824 or 1825, after an orgy of spending – buying property willy-nilly, gambling and debauching – he was bankrupted and it is believed he probably fled the country as Philip Sheppard had before him. When the tale was recounted to Philip by A.T. Playne's grandfather, Philip is reputed to have exclaimed at Whitehead's 'cleverness' – it had, after all, taken Philip thirteen *years* to get through about the same sum of money!

William Playne of nearby Longfords, who came of a well-established clothier family, acquired the manor of

An ornate clock tells the time above windows which have been re-shaped since Storer's view

Avening in 1812. David Ricardo (1772–1823), who had made a fortune on the London Stock Exchange, bought the manor of Minchinhampton and Gatcombe Park in 1814. The connection of common ownership which had bound the two manors together for more than seven centuries was thus finally broken.

David Ricardo was the third child of a Dutch Jew who had settled in London and made money on the Stock Exchange. At the age of fourteen, David was employed in his father's business, although later he set up his own. He published many pamphlets and became the main founder of what has been called the classical school of political economy. He retired from business a year after he acquired the Gatcombe estate, although he was still active in the community at large. He became Sheriff in 1818 and early in 1819 he became Member of Parliament for the Irish borough of Portarlington. It is probable that he actually bought the borough, as he had never even been to Ireland, but he held the seat until he died in 1823.

David Ricardo, eminent political economist, or according to Cobbett, 'a boroughmonger, of all God's creatures, the basest', bought Gatcombe in 1814

Ricardo was not only wealthy and well-esteemed professionally, he was also a great benefactor. The *Dictionary of National Biography* reports that he contributed to nearly every London charity and that he gave support, too, to an almshouse and two schools in the neighbourhood of Gatcombe.

He also appears to have been well-liked and a generous-natured man: life at the 'delightfully pleasant house' of Gatcombe, as described by a visitor, Miss Edgeworth, in her *Life and Letters*, sounds relaxed and informal, with Ricardo entertaining his guest with charades and charming conversation.

It was at Gatcombe that Ricardo was taken ill and died, leaving a widow and three sons and four daughters. The

eldest son, Osman, succeeded to the estate of Bromes-
berrow, Gloucestershire, the second, David, inherited
Gatcombe, and the third, Mortimer, made his way as a
captain in the 2nd Lifeguards.

David Ricardo was buried in Hardenhuish churchyard
and a curious tale is recorded by Kilvert in his *Diary* about
the monument which was set on the tomb there. Ricardo
himself had ordered the monument, to a design, incorporat-
ing four figures, which he had brought back with him from a

Kilvert's *Diary* tells of
Ricardo's curious tomb in
Hardenhuish churchyard and
recounts a strange story of
how he was cheated by the
sculptor

tomb in Rome. The price paid for the monument was £2,000 and it should have been made in marble, but when it started to shale off, it was discovered to be made of a composition. In subsequent winters the figures had to be protected against frost by being boarded up. 'The sculptor, Mr Pitts,' Kilvert writes, 'destroyed himself afterwards.'

About three years after David Ricardo II (1803–64) succeeded to Gatcombe, William Cobbett made one of his *Rural Rides* from Malmesbury to Stroud via Tetbury and Avening. His notes give another good picture of Gatcombe at the time – as well as the manner in which Cobbett viewed its previous owner. He had come to the edge of the high land and was looking down upon the village of Avening, and he recorded:

seeing, just close to it, a large fine mansion-house, a beautiful park, and, making part of the park, one of the finest, most magnificent woods (of 200 acres, I dare say) lying facing me, going from a valley up a gently-rising hill. While I was sitting on my horse, admiring the spot, a man came along with some tools in his hand, as if he were going somewhere to work as a plumber. 'Whose beautiful place is that?' said I. 'One "Squire Ricardo", I think they call him.' You might have knocked me down with a feather. . . .

Cobbett called in at the Cross Inn, Avening, and was told that Gatcombe had belonged to a Mr Sheppard and to his fathers before him. 'I asked', Cobbett subsequently wrote, 'where this Sheppard was now. A tradesman-looking man told me that he did not know where he was; but that he had heard he was living somewhere near Bath! Thus they go!

Gatcombe in its setting at the head of a narrow valley leading down to the Avening stream

The restoration of Minchinhampton Church (*far left*), the building of Amberley Church (*left*) and fund-raising for Brimscombe Church (*below*) owed much to the generosity of the second David Ricardo

Thus they are squeezed out of existence.' Ricardo, he considered, was a 'boroughmonger', of all God's creatures, the basest.

Cobbett, who held radical views, would have known that Ricardo once represented in Parliament the twelve electors of the Irish rotten borough of Portarlington.

If David Ricardo I bought his political position, it is only fair to note that two of his sons became MPs in a more conventional manner. Osman was MP for Worcester 1847–65 and David II was MP for Stroud 1832–3. Although the latter was a short period of office, it is memorable because David, together with W.H. Hyett of Painswick, was the first representative of the new borough.

David Ricardo II was a great benefactor to the manor of Minchinhampton. He was Chairman of the Stroud Board of Guardians until 1856 and he built Amberley Church in 1836, starting a school in its basement. He also contributed £2,000 towards the restoration of Minchinhampton Church in 1842. When there were calls in the late 1830s for a church to be built to serve the 1,452 inhabitants of Brimscombe, it

was Ricardo who led the way to raising the money, personally contributing a large amount of the £2,000 it cost.

Brimscombe Church was built in a period when the Oxford Movement and its 'high church' views held great sway in the country. Ricardo, though, expressed the opinion that Brimscombe Church should demonstrate the Protestant and Reformation tradition of the Church of England. That his opinion was respected can be seen in the construction of the church: the sanctuary and chancel, for example, are at the west end of the building and not the east end.

The church was consecrated in 1840, and a *Gloucester Journal* report of the time noted that 'near the church are built two excellent schoolrooms, capable of receiving, at least, 200 boys and girls'.

Ricardo's close association with all three churches continued throughout his life, since the gift of the living of Minchinhampton, consisting of Minchinhampton and the district churches of Amberley and Brimscombe, was in his hands (purchased by his father and passed on to him).

David II was succeeded by his son Henry David (1833–73), after whose death trustees held the manor until the coming of age of his son Henry George (1860–1940).

Henry George Ricardo was educated at Winchester and the Royal Military Academy, Woolwich, and duly commissioned in the Royal Artillery. He retired about 1897. With the outbreak of the First World War in August 1914, it was reported that in Stroud:

there were animated scenes in the yard of the Midland Railway Company, where horses were being brought in from all directions for inspection by the buying officers. About thirty mounts were purchased for the Ninth

Lieutenant-Colonel Henry George Ricardo was the third Ricardo to own Gatcombe. Here he is photographed (seated) with his three brothers, all of them aged over fifty and serving in the First World War

Lancers by Major Ricardo, and about fifty for the Yeomanry.

Returning to the army, Ricardo found himself in France where in June 1916 he was mentioned in despatches and in January 1917 awarded the Distinguished Service Order. During the war he was photographed with his three brothers, all over fifty years of age – Rear Admiral Arthur David Ricardo, RN, Captain William Cowley Ricardo of the Canadian Army and Brigadier General Ambrose St Quintin

Ricardo, CMG, DSO – by which time Henry George Ricardo had been promoted lieutenant-colonel.

Both before and after the war Colonel Ricardo became immersed in public life. He was chairman of the Nailsworth bench of magistrates, for twelve years a county councillor, and for twenty-four president of the Mid-Gloucestershire Conservative Association. At Minchinhampton he was a churchwarden and a parish councillor, and he was the first president of Minchinhampton Golf Club, which was formed in 1889.

By 1913 he had sold his rights in Minchinhampton Common to the National Trust after increased quarrying had caused alarm. As the Second World War approached he found the financial burden of the upkeep of Gatcombe becoming increasingly onerous. Gloucester Lunatic Asylum made an offer of £22,500 for its purchase for the rehousing of patients.

When news of this offer broke, quite a storm blew up involving Colonel Ricardo and his neighbours Lord Lee of Fareham and his wife Ruth. Lord Lee, best remembered for his gift of Chequers to the nation as a residence for the prime minister, had recently retired permanently to Old Quarries, Avening, adjacent to the Gatcombe estate. There, he was devoting much of his time to the creation of a gallery for his collections of art – later to be used to store some 230 pictures from the National Gallery during the war.

When he got wind of the proposal to sell Gatcombe to the lunatic asylum he was not at all pleased. The episode is recorded with great feeling in his private papers, collected under the title *A Good Innings*. He felt that Ricardo, an old brother-officer, was acting in a way which showed a callous indifference to his neighbours – threatening both their

Chequers, bequeathed to the nation by Lord Lee. He also managed to prevent the sale of Gatcombe to Gloucester Lunatic Asylum when Ricardo found it too expensive to maintain

An Edwardian view of the
entrance to Gatcombe

peace and quiet (because Lord Lee feared the prevalent
treatment of allowing patients to wander about freely would
lead to awkward encounters in the fields and lanes) and also
the value of their properties. Most of all, he was outraged by
the fact that he thought Ricardo had been conducting the
deal surreptitiously.

As it happened, Samuel Courtauld, a great friend of Lord
Lee (chairman of Courtaulds Ltd, 1921–46), was visiting
him on the weekend of the gloomy news. Finding the couple
so downcast he offered to buy Gatcombe, which he said
would make a sound investment. At Courtauld's bidding,
Lord Lee immediately offered to purchase Gatcombe 'himself' – cash down and for the same price quoted by the
asylum – and after tense negotiations Ricardo agreed. 'Thus
the great battle concluded' Lord Lee wrote. Thus also,
Gatcombe came under the Courtauld aegis.

Gatcombe Park became the country home of Samuel
Courtauld and when he died in 1947 he bequeathed it,
along with the farm attached to it, to his son-in-law
R.A. 'Rab' Butler, often called the greatest Prime Minister
the country never had.

Rab had already spent time at Gatcombe with his wife Mollie, visiting his father-in-law, most notably in the summer recess of 1940, when the peace and quiet of the Gloucestershire countryside must have provided a welcome respite from the war and work in the Foreign Office – and from personal attacks against him over his alleged attitude of appeasement, based on remarks he had reportedly made to a Swedish minister.

Rab was kept away from his new property of Gatcombe by his busy political schedule, so he left the land to be looked after by a farm manager and the house by a small staff. He tried to let the house, but without great success, and for a while it was used as a 'rest home' by senior executives from Courtaulds.

There were, however, at least two sensitive occasions in his life when he retreated to Gatcombe. The first occurred in 1963 at one of the moments when Rab almost became Prime Minister. Harold Macmillan was ill and it was expected by many people that Rab, as Deputy Prime Minister, would make the obvious choice to succeed him. Yet, as a result of a certain amount of manoeuvring, Alec, Lord Home was called upon to step into Macmillan's shoes, and, in spite of the huge disappointment, Rab agreed to serve under him. In her memoir *August and Rab*, Mollie recalled the gloomy train journey which took them both away to the Gloucestershire countryside (which could only refer to Gatcombe). It was no doubt again a welcome sanctuary from the immediate political furore.

The second occasion noted in Mollie's memoir recalls a more pleasant episode. In 1965 Rab was offered the place of Master of Trinity College, Cambridge by Harold Wilson. It would mean leaving politics and, at the age of sixty-two,

As this early photograph shows, the main drive to the house used to run up through the valley; now it has been re-sited to approach discreetly from the side

Today the view from the
house remains unrivalled.
The grazing sheep, the woods
and the distant Cotswold hills
must be much as they were
when William Cobbett
admired this beautiful setting
in his *Rural Rides*

Rab was undecided. He was also being offered a life
peerage. He spent a good while thinking about it, but
eventually came to a decision. When he posted his letter of
acceptance, it was put in a pillar box at Gatcombe. Had the
weekend spent there helped him finally to clarify his
thoughts? Mollie certainly says that Rab was very fond of
the place, always enjoying the country scene, the farm and
the sheep, and chatting to the farm manager.

Once installed at Trinity, Lord Butler of Saffron Walden
did not, however, have any more time than previously to
visit Gatcombe: he and Mollie made the three-hour journey
there only twice a term. Eventually, approaching his mid-
seventies and with the end of his appointment at Trinity in

sight, Lord Butler began to think about where he would retire. It was not to Gatcombe, but to Spencers in Essex, which had been Mollie's home with her first husband, August. Gatcombe was sold to the Queen as a home for the Princess Royal in 1976, for an estimated £500,000. Lord Butler thought, so Patrick Cosgrave records in *R.A. Butler: An English Life*, that the royal family drove a very hard bargain!

Mollie had always considered the house too big for her and Rab, and Rab, too, felt that the running of the estate had become too much for him. Nevertheless it was with regret that they gave it up, although with pleasure, too, at the thought of its new owner.

Reports of the sale described an estate which included a 12-acre trout lake, 530 acres of farmland, 200 acres of woodland, stables, farm buildings, four cottages, and also, so it was said, a phantom headless black hound which some locals claimed roamed along the Minchinhampton to Avening road.

At the time the farmland was divided between arable, used to grow crops such as wheat and barley, and pasture for a beef breeding herd and cows. The acreage of farmland has since more than doubled, with further purchases of surrounding land and the development of the farming enterprise.

Use has also been made of the commoners' right to graze cattle and horses on the 600-acre Minchinhampton Common for a small payment per animal. The right has been jealously guarded to avoid the fate of many other commons which have been enclosed, particularly towards the end of the eighteenth century. Anyone living within the parish of Minchinhampton used to qualify for the

In recent years the annual
horse trials have become a
major equestrian event,
attracting top names and
affording the public a rare
opportunity to view the estate

commoners' right but this changed with the Commons
Registration Act of 1965. Anyone who did not register lost
their right. Fortunately, all owners of Gatcombe Park
qualify. Registered commoners take their beasts to be
tagged on marking day in May – cattle have ear tags and
horses are branded on the hoof – and then they leave their
animals to graze the common. The right is not just exer-
cised to maintain a tradition, it is recognized as a valuable
economic asset to those who keep cattle and horses.

Initially when the Butlers left Gatcombe there was much
redecorating and renovating to be done to the house, which
had become run down. It is interesting to note in this
respect that the Princess Royal had actually looked at and
rejected Highgrove in favour of Gatcombe, even though the

latter would require more repairs. The house was rewired and replumbed and there were major interior structural alterations carried out, such as changes of use of rooms on the first floor: the bedrooms, for example, situated to the rear of the house, which was darker, were brought to the front where occupants could have a splendid view of the valley below and enjoy more sunshine. An entire nursery suite was created in the attics, which had in earlier times been used mainly by servants. Downstairs, less was altered, leaving the rooms much as they were when Gatcombe Park was built.

Outside, there have been renovations to the conservatory, and the stable facilities, which were not actually being used for horses in 1976, have been improved beyond measure. This was essential for the development of an equestrian centre at Gatcombe Park. Since 1983, Gatcombe has been famous for its annual summer horse trials.

Over the years, the trials have attracted the top names from equestrian circles from the UK and overseas. Winners have included competitors such as the Olympic gold medallist Mark Todd, David Green, Bruce Davidson, Robert Lemieux and Mary Thomson. But the event has not just been about cross-country, dressage and show-jumping. Each year there have been exciting diversions to entertain the crowds which flock to the estate: a Land-Rover celebrity race, sheep-dog and gun-dog trials, displays by local branches of Riding For The Disabled, gymnastic displays, military bands and many other spectacles. On such occasions the general public have a rare opportunity to visit and enjoy this beautiful estate. Gatcombe Park is normally a quieter place and the house is essentially a private home.

The Garden at Gatcombe Park

BY ROSEMARY VEREY

Mature natural woodland forms a perfect backdrop to the weathered stonework of the house

In the garden the Princess Royal is helped by Mr Eric Hanshett, who first came to Gatcombe in 1956 to work as a forester and is now in charge of garden maintenance. His first love is trees, and this is reflected in the sensitive way in which the lawn gradually gives way to the natural woodland. Sumachs, a specimen *Acer griseum*, a weeping white mulberry and cornus, viburnums and hollies (presents to the Princess Royal) are integrated into the beech trees.

Winter jasmine and wistaria
flank the central portico

The house façade is clothed with well-trained winter jasmine and wistaria, and from under the portico on the front door steps there is an utterly satisfying view. Beyond a wide flat terrace of gravel and grass and a curving stone balustrade, the ground slopes away sharply. There is a timelessness about this valley, with a stream which suddenly appears above ground, dammed sometime in the last century to create a small lake or pool – now dark water surrounded by alder trees. The stream trickles on and two more pools have been formed in this perfect amphitheatre, the setting for the sport which the Princess Royal enjoys – eventing. The obstacles built for the equestrian events appear natural.

A lion's head looks out across
the valley from the curving
stone balustrade

Nicotianas and fuchsias thrive under the gently curving glass of the conservatory

I asked Mr Hanshett the inevitable question, 'Is the Princess Royal interested in her garden?' His answer, full of understanding, was, 'Yes. Her Royal Highness always notices and appreciates what has been done.' There is a time for everything, and gardening often complements an active devotion to horses. Man's handling of his horse throughout history has been as much a cultivated skill as the art of gardening.

The farmland, grazing horses, managed woodland, and above all the green Cotswold hills combine to make a perfect setting. The grandeur of Gatcombe is created by nature and should have no further enhancement.

Nether Lypiatt

 Nether Lypiatt Manor, or Lower Lypiatt Hall, or the Haunted House, as it has been called at various times, became the home of Prince and Princess of Michael of Kent in 1980.

Nether Lypiatt, between Bisley and Stroud, is situated, like Gatcombe Park, in an area which is rich in ancient remains such as neolithic barrows and flints. The old names of fields in the region, recorded in the Tithe Terrier, evoke a colourful past: Langstone (1454) suggests some prehistoric stone monument, for example, whereas Roman Camp Piece (1378) points to the presence of the invaders. Roman coins and artefacts have also been discovered further to support this evidence.

The actual name Lypiatt (known at different times as Lippiatt, Lippyate, Lopegat, Lupegate, etc.) derives from the Anglo-Saxon period and the words *hlyp*, to jump, and *yat*, a gate. Hence, Lypiatt originally signified a leapgate, or a low gate which was constructed in woods or forests. This gate was built to a height given by forest law, which allowed deer to leap over it but would keep sheep from straying. Farming and agriculture would, of course, have been the

occupation of many in the area until the rise of the clothiers and the Cotswold woollen industry, which prospered from the sixteenth century until the mid-nineteenth century. A great number of local inhabitants then made their living from the mills which sprang up, particularly in the Stroud valleys where there were over 150 mills by the early nineteenth century.

From the thirteenth century, the manor of Nether Lypiatt was the property of the Ream or Freame family. Records of the de Reom, atte Reome, Reem, Ream, Freme or Freame family (as it was called over successive generations) are scant, but local historian Stan Gardiner believes the family could well have been of Norman origin, since John de Reom is recorded as holding half a knight's fee in 1349. This would have been a type of tenancy and could have derived from an ancestor coming to England under William the Conqueror. Often, knights would have been akin to lords of the manor of Norman villages and William would have given them something equivalent in England in return for their services to him. By the sixteenth century there were more records of the Freame family, who, the Bisley Parish registers make it clear (if any such evidence were needed), were well-to-do gentlefolk.

The last direct male heir, Thomas Freame, died in 1664. He left three heiresses, the eldest of whom, Ann (baptized 1635), married Thomas Chamberlayne of Wanborough, Wiltshire. Their daughter, Catherine, married Charles Coxe and she brought to him the manor of Nether Lypiatt.

A member of a Rodmarton family, of which place he was subsequently Lord of the Manor, Charles Coxe had a distinguished career as puisne judge of sessions for Brecknock, Glamorgan and Radnor 1702–4 and chief justice

Nether Lypiatt Manor – 'the perfect grand house in miniature' there 1704–14. He was MP for Cirencester 1693–1705 and 1708–13 and for Gloucester 1713–22. He was also clerk of the patent office in London.

The Freames had lived in a house or mansion at Nether Lypiatt, next to the site of the current Manor, from 1509. At various times over the years pieces of its foundations have been discovered and it was known that there was a well there. When an earth excavator was levelling the field next to the manor for Princess Michael several years ago, the well was uncovered. It had been made of cut stone and was over 60 feet deep. A small wall has now been built around it and it is open to view.

Like the present manor the old house, Princess Michael says, was known as the 'haunted house', although the

The restored well, a legacy from an earlier manor

The 'Haunted House', a description which has attached itself to Nether Lypiatt down the centuries, as in the caption to this old postcard

Nether Lypiatt Manor from the north-east prior to restoration (*left*). Note the absence of the dormer windows, now reinstated (*below*). The south front (*over*) with its two pavilions displays a perfect symmetry

reason for this is not known. Princess Michael suggests that it could simply have been that its size and situation on the top of the Lypiatt ridge gave it a forbidding aspect which led to tales and rumours growing up. In any case, Judge Coxe destroyed it and built the mansion much as it is today.

Miss Mary Rudd in her *Historical Records of Bisley* says the house is built of oolite stone said to have been quarried in Bisley, and consists of a barrel-vaulted cellar, a basement floor with entrances to north and south, with two storeys of the chief rooms and an attic with a single-span hipped roof, which had two dormer windows on every side until 1848, when the house was practically re-roofed and they were removed. Subsequent restorations have replaced them. The date 1717 is to be seen on the rainwater heads of lead, with the Coxe crest, a crowing cock.

This date has frequently been quoted as that of

completion of the house, yet Princess Michael possesses a table inlaid with ivory, made in 1703, which portrays the manor. It must, therefore, have been finished, or at least substantially finished, by this earlier date. Princess Michael's own researches further suggest that the building of the house began around 1690.

The forecourt to the manor and the road from Brimscombe are separated by ornate gates. It was along this road that Charles I travelled in the Civil War to undertake the siege of Gloucester. The occasion is recorded in Paul Hawkins Fisher's *Notes and Recollections of Stroud*. The army on 8 August 1643, he wrote:

> marched from Bristol to Tetbury, a distance of twenty miles; where his Majesty dined, and then proceeded to Cirencester to Sir William Master's 'to supper and bed'. On the next day, the army proceeded to Hampton Road (as Minchinhampton was sometimes called because there the great high roads from Bath to Gloucester, and from Cirencester to the passage of the Severn at Newnham, met, and crossed each other) and descended into the Stroud valley at Brimscombe. Here they crossed the river Froom; and, ascending the steep south side of Stroud hill by way of Quar-house, passed directly in front of Lypiatt Hall.

The fine stone piers and wrought-ironwork are among the many features which earn this house its Grade I listing

There is a legend that Judge Coxe sentenced to death a smith for murder (or, some say, for sheep-stealing), but pardoned him on condition that he made the gates for his rebuilt house. However, as soon as the gates were completed, the judge retracted the reprieve, and this has given rise to the supposed haunting of the property, both inside

The wrought-iron gates at Nether Lypiatt are at the root of the story about its supposed haunting

and outside the house. Every year, on 25 January, the anniversary of the execution, the gates are said inexplicably to sweep open at midnight – to allow in the vengeance-seeking blacksmith.

There appears to be absolutely no foundation in truth whatever to this story. Miss Rudd says that the gates were thought to be the work of Warren of Cambridge, a well-known artificer who made gates at that period – for example, at Trinity College, Cambridge and Burleigh House, Enfield. In fact, she notes, there was a close resemblance between the gates of the latter and those at Nether Lypiatt. In any case, the gates at Nether Lypiatt could not have been the work of a simple local blacksmith. Mr John Stanton, whose father once owned the property, confirms that the original gates were repaired by Messrs Chew of Stroud. The screen of stone piers, linked by wrought-iron grilles, and with the very fine wrought-iron gates, divided the inner from the outer courtyard. It is one of the many remarkable features of the house for which it is listed Grade I. A recent owner sought to close this clairvoyee by building another wall in front. The local authority's objection was upheld by the Department of the Environment and the wall had to be removed.

Nether Lypiatt Manor is the perfect grand house in miniature. Sir Sacheverell Sitwell has written:

> no house could compose so beautifully for a glass transparency, with wrought iron gates in front flanked by a pair of little formal pavilions, and with an interior where music will forever linger, for it was the home of Violet Gordon Woodhouse.

Two columns and a flight of thirteen steps provide a grand entrance to the house

Mrs Woodhouse, an early broadcaster and well-known player of the clavichord and harpsichord, lived in the manor with her husband from 1923. Lord Barrington also lived there with them and is known to have made the garden exceedingly beautiful. The combination of her music and the beauty of the place created a lasting impression on eveyone privileged to visit.

Architecturally the house is of great importance as the elevations of the main building are clearly derived from those at Coleshill (built about fifty years earlier and now demolished). The large central chimney stack is intended to take the place of the belvedere or lantern in larger houses, such as

The memorial to Judge
Coxe's extraordinary horse
stands on a very exposed
slope in this early photograph
of the estate

Coleshill which Judge Coxe must often have passed on his way
to London. The house is only 46 feet square, but it has a modest
English version of the *piano nobile*. Internally the plan is
ingenious. All the features of the principal rooms had survived
when the 'Buildings of England' volume on *The Cotswolds* was
published in 1970, though the attic floor had been reconstructed by P. Morley Horder. The principal staircase starts
as a dog-leg stair, but by means of off-sets in the wall it widens
gradually until at the top it is of open-well form. The porch has
two detached fluted columns supporting a segmental pediment approached up a flight of thirteen steps.

Wings stand corner to corner with the house to the
north-west (roof added by P. Morley Horder in 1923),
south-west, and south-east. All the buildings are faced in
Cotswold ashlar of admirable quality and roofed with
Cotswold stone slates.

Judge Coxe's building was not just restricted to the
manor. P.H. Fisher records the erection in Lower Lypiatt
Wood by the judge of an obelisk in memory of a favourite
horse which died in 1721. The monument originally had an

iron plaque on the base, but this was removed and lost. However, the inscription, recalled by Mrs Ridler, the wife of a later tenant of the farm, and noted by Miss Rudd was:

My name was Wag, that rolled the green,
The oldest horse that ever was seen,
My years they numbered forty-two –
I served my master just and true.

The plaque was replaced in 1936. Wag must have been an extraordinary horse. He was sent off to walk to Stroud by himself with a shopping list in his pannier. He would stop at the shops required so that his bags could be filled before returning home again. Memorials to Judge Coxe, by comparison, are small, the only local note of his death in 1729 being a brief entry in the Rodmarton burial register. (Compare with this, too, the several monuments at Rodmarton which were dedicated to his brother and to his own descendants.)

There is an even more curious postscript to the monument in that a horse belonging to Judge Coxe is said to haunt the staircase of the manor. Is the horse Wag? And why should the horse appear on the staircase? The origin of the haunting legend is even more mysterious than that of the blacksmith.

Nether Lypiatt Manor and also a farm at Tarlton, Coates, was left by Judge Coxe to his son John (1696–1783), a barrister who was MP for Cirencester 1749–54. He left to his grandson Charles his manors of Rodmarton and Hayley and lands in Sapperton, Oddington, Avening, Stroud and Bisley. It seems unlikely that John spent much time at Nether Lypiatt, however. As Miss Rudd points out, he is known to have been one of the feoffees of Rodborough of land held by

Now hidden among the trees, Wag's obelisk still pays tribute to a horse which is supposed to have run errands to Stroud with no assistance but a shopping list

them in Bisley, yet there is little record of him found in connection with any events at Bisley, beyond the witnessing of a deed. When John died, his son Charles inherited Nether Lypiatt.

In 1749 Charles Coxe II married Elizabeth, a daughter and eventual co-heir of Sir Robert Westley, Lord Mayor of London in 1743. They had one son, Charles Westley Coxe of Kemble House, who became MP for North Wiltshire. In his turn he inherited his father's manors, including Nether Lypiatt, and from his mother the manors of Poole Keynes.

Charles Westley Coxe was married in 1789 to Ann, daughter of Robert Gordon of Auchendolly. They had one child, a daughter called Elizabeth Anne. Charles died in 1806, with Elizabeth Anne his only heir and she succeeded to all his estates. She married her cousin Robert Gordon (d. 1865) of Auchendolly and of Lewiston House, Dorset. They had one daughter, Anna, who was born in 1809.

The Bisley Tithe Terrior of 1841 shows that at this period, during the continuing ownership of Nether Lypiatt by the Gordon family, the land was tenanted. It is interesting to note a business transaction recorded from this period. Kemble was on the planned route of the railway line from Swindon to Cheltenham and in 1836 Gordon was paid £7,500 as 'compensation for damage to be sustained'. He also demanded that the railway should be in a covered way where it passed Kemble House. This explains the tunnel, 415 yards long, which exists to this day. He also stipulated that there should be no public station on the estate and it was not until 1879, when a director of the Great Western, with about twenty other passengers, finding himself herded in a small shed in bitter cold, opened negotiations with Gordon's only daughter and heir Anna that one was built.

The lawn mower was invented by Edwin Budding at Thrupp in 1830. Ransome and May's catalogue of 1851 illustrates it in front of Nether Lypiatt Manor

For many years Nether Lypiatt was tenanted by farmers – here the front garden is being used to shear sheep around the time of the First World War

She made a stipulation that there should be no refreshment room for the sale of alcohol.

Anna Gordon (1809–84) left her manors, apart from Nether Lypiatt, to Michael Biddulph of Ledbury, a great friend of her father (in accordance with his wishes). In 1882 she gave Nether Lypiatt by deed of gift to a cousin, Philip Charles Sheppard, a son of the extravagant Philip, last Sheppard to own Gatcombe Park before he fled his creditors in 1812. Mr Stan Gardiner has worked out their relationship as follows: Charles Coxe II of Kemble House, whose daughter married Edward Sheppard, builder of Gatcombe, would have been great-grandfather of both Philip Charles Sheppard and of Anna Gordon. Philip Charles and Anna were, therefore, second cousins. In giving Nether Lypiatt to Philip Charles, Anna was carrying out the provision of her grandmother's will – notably in her own lifetime, not at her death. She also presented to Gloucester College of Art three fine pieces of tapestry of late seventeenth-century work, which had adorned one of the bedrooms.

Nether Lypiatt Manor itself was tenanted for many years by farmers. William Gardner (1730–1812), of Scottish descent, held it for several years. He married Mary Capner of Bisley in 1758 and they raised ten children.

In 1812 it was leased to George Ridler. George's great-great-grandson, Jack Ridler, provides the following information regarding the succession of tenants at the Manor: George Ridler, baptized at Bisley in 1762, obtained the lease at Nether Lypiatt Manor until his death there in 1837. He bequeathed the interest in the manor lease to the two youngest of his eleven children, Robert and Jane. Robert died in 1845, aged thirty-five. Jane had married Charles Ractliffe, who farmed at Abnash, the year before, and they then moved to the manor, where, presumably, their first child, George Robert Ridler Ractliffe, was born in 1846.

By 1851, the Ractliffes had had a second child, Ann Ridler Ractliffe, and they were farming some 200 acres at the manor and employing five labourers. George Ractliffe, their son, went to his father's farm at Stancombe Ash some time around the 1870s. Charles Ractliffe senior had 160 acres there in 1851 and was helped by two other unmarried sons.

Jane Ractliffe (née Ridler) died in 1876 at Nether Lypiatt Manor. The lease continued via her daughter (and George's sister), Elizabeth Jane, who had married William Thomas Wallis. Their son, Charles Pearson Wallis then took on the farming until around 1915. At this point, the connected tenancy of over a hundred years which had started with George Ridler was broken.

At Nether Lypiatt, garden and house combine to produce an endless variety of vistas

The property, being in the hands of mortgagees, was sold to Arthur William Stanton (1875–1944) before the First World War. He was the son of Walter John Stanton, a woollen manufacturer, who was MP for Stroud, February to May 1874 (when he was unseated on petition) and 1880–5. A.W. Stanton also contested several Parliamentary elections, but unsuccessfully.

A.W. Stanton never resided at the manor because he went to live at Field Place, Paganhill, which he had inherited from a bachelor uncle. When he bought Nether Lypiatt Manor, however, it had been his intention to restore it, as by this time it badly needed repairs. To this end he employed the architect Percy Morley Horder (1870–1944) to prepare plans for its occupation, and some of the more urgent repairs, including the gates, were carried out.

In 1919 Nether Lypiatt was acquired by Corbett W. Woodall, a restorer of many ancient houses, and with the assistance of Morley Horder a complete and most satisfactory restoration was effected.

Morley Horder was a colourful man, known for his excessive artistic temperament, yet his work was very well respected. A fair amount of his work was carried out in the Cotswolds, such as traditional stonework houses at Stinchcombe, Stroud, Dursley and Pitchford, and the Gyde Orphanage near Painswick. He was also connected locally through his marriage in 1897 to Rosa Catherine, the daughter of one Ebenezer Apperly, a dental surgeon of Stroud.

At Nether Lypiatt, Morley Horder reconstructed the attic floor and added the roof of one of the wings, as detailed earlier in describing the appearance of the house. Work during this time also led to two interesting discoveries.

The south side of Nether Lypiatt Manor showing initial stages in its restoration: (*left*) the dormer windows have been replaced, the lean-to removed and blind windows re-opened. A comparison with pages 98–9 shows the achievements of subsequent restoration

Bones discovered beneath the site of a new tennis court featured in the *Cheltenham Chronicle and Gloucester Graphic* in 1919

One, reported in the *Stroud News* of 5 December, 1919, involved the uncovering of bones in the garden at the manor. Part of the garden was being levelled in preparation for the creation of a tennis court. Just 2 or 3 feet below the surface of the garden, skeletons were found buried vertically with their feet together, believed to be those of men about 6 feet tall.

Unfortunately, experts do not seem to have been called in to examine the skeletons and record the exact positions in which they were found, although local historian F.T. Hammond, in his notes to Miss Rudd's *Historical Records of Bisley*, states that he visited the scene a few days after the discovery. It had been reported that seven skeletons were found, although the facts were never confirmed, and when Mr Hammond arrived, he was shown a heap of bones covered over with a sheet of corrugated iron. He was allowed to take away part of a jaw bone from one of the skeletons, which he examined (and subsequently passed to Stroud Museum). The only conclusion of note was that the teeth on the jaw bone were worn flat, indicating a diet of coarse food. Mr Walrond of Stroud Museum asserted that the bones had been thrown into a pig-sty during work on the tennis court and that all that remained afterwards was a chewed skull or jaw-bone (the one now in Stroud Museum).

The *Stroud News* concluded that the bones were from soldiers killed in the Civil War and that they could not be traced back to prehistoric times. But as Miss Rudd points out, there is no record of there having been any skirmishes at Nether Lypiatt (although there was fighting at Over Lypiatt). It was also customary that those killed in fighting were given a proper Christian burial in a churchyard, unless the encounter was a huge battle with many dead. The fact, too, that the teeth were worn down in the manner described by Mr Hammond would imply that the skeletons could well have been of more ancient origins than the Civil War.

A second discovery, of an heraldic stone, was made inside the house during restoration work carried out in 1922. Again Mr Hammond collected details of the find: it is thought that the stone, measuring approximately 2 feet square and 4 inches thick, was a remnant of the old house which Judge Coxe had pulled down. When uncovered, the

The mysterious heraldic stone combining the arms of three local families – a remnant of the old house hidden in the walls of the new one

shield was facing inwards and must have been used as building material in the new Manor.

The shield is curious for the fact that it combines the coats of arms of three families, Freame, Bigge and Query. The Freame–Bigge relationship can be traced back to the marriage between Thomas Freame (d. 1659/60), eldest son of the Freames of Nether Lypiatt, and Elizabeth (d. 1647), daughter of Thomas Bigge of Lenchwick, Worcestershire. Their son Thomas, the last direct male of the Freame family, married Ann Query (d. 1694) and their arms were impaled, which showed the families had come together. As their marriage took place about 1631 and Thomas died in 1664, it would suggest the shield was put up between those two dates, possibly soon after the marriage.

When the shield was found in 1922, it was reset over the fireplace in the dining-room, although Mr Woodall had it removed shortly afterwards because he wanted to put panelling into the room. For a while it was stored away, then it was removed from the manor to The Chantry at Bisley. The coat of arms now resides there.

After the restoration work had been carried out, Woodall sold the property to Mr and Mrs Gordon Woodhouse in 1923. Its subsequent owners were her nephew, John Gwynne, Frederick Nettlefold, Major Barrington and Mr and Mrs Simon Boyle, who purchased the manor for £100,000 in 1976.

It was while Suna Boyle, half-sister of Viscount Portman, and her husband Simon, an entrepreneur and designer, lived at Nether Lypiatt that there was an attempt to improve the privacy of the manor by building a wall in front of the railings. Since the railings and clairvoyee are considered outstanding features of the manor, it is not sur-

The stable block, one of a range of attractive Cotswold outbuildings

prising that their work was met with immediate opposition from the local authorities. The Boyles had spent around £50,000 on renovations since they moved in, including the cost of the Cotswold stone wall. But at a public inquiry it was decided the wall would have to be removed.

Public attention was further attracted to Nether Lypiatt Manor when it was reported that an exorcism had taken place there at the request of the Boyles. The Reverend Ian Hazlewood of Prestbury, who was called in to perform the exorcism, recalls over ten years later that 'there was a presence there, a soul that hadn't left this world'. The episode led to a revitalization, with some degree of embellishment, of the blacksmith legend. By now, the blacksmith appeared sometimes headless and sometimes riding a white horse around the courtyard, a confusion perhaps with the alleged haunting of the stairs by Judge Coxe's horse. There was also a tale of a mysterious woman dressed in white who was said to haunt the grounds.

No such legends discouraged Prince and Princess Michael of Kent from recognizing the outstanding attractiveness of the manor. In Princess Michael's words, the front 'looks like a dolls' house'. Nor were they deterred by the fact that, with a main block measuring 46 feet square, the house was small by royal standards. The manor became theirs for a reported £300,000 in 1980.

The details of the property which had been circulated by the estate agents described Nether Lypiatt as a country house with four reception rooms, a studio, eight bedrooms, four bathrooms, two dressing rooms, a staff wing, utility rooms, cellars, garaging and farm buildings, including a tithe barn with planning permission. The grounds contained a tennis court, heated swimming pool and formal gardens, three paddocks and woodland amounting to 35 acres (over the years, portions of the land originally pertaining to the manor had been sold off, greatly reducing the acreage).

Since acquiring Nether Lypiatt, Prince and Princess Michael have been very busy carrying out renovations and improvements to the manor and converting outbuildings for use by staff.

In addition to the necessary rewiring and attention to plumbing, several aesthetic improvements to the exterior of the house have been effected. On the north side windows had been blocked in with cement, a frequent practice in years gone by to avoid window tax, but one which gave to the house a rather bleak and forbidding aspect. The solution arrived at was to paint in the windows and put lead over them to make them look like real windows. 'The effect was so convincing,' Princess Michael says, 'that the council asked us if we had had planning permission to re-open the windows!'

Beneath the windows a further improvement was made

The north face of the house has been greatly improved by painting in windows which had been blocked to avoid window tax (compare with the photograph on page 97)

Ashdown House, its
dimensions strikingly similar
to those of Nether Lypiatt

with the construction of a stone portico, a copy of the one over the front door but somewhat less formal in style. The new portico replaced a fire escape which had been both unsightly and impractical.

On the east side, a wooden balcony has been installed on the first floor, above the cellar, although due to the gradient of the land on which the house is built, it is at the same level as the entrance steps to the front. The story behind this addition is intriguing and possibly throws more light on the original building of the manor. Princess Michael had noticed a striking similarity between the exterior dimensions of Nether Lypiatt and Ashdown House, Lambourn, now owned by the National Trust. This seventeenth-century house was built by the First Lord Craven and consecrated to Elizabeth, Queen of Bohemia. Princess Michael believes that either Judge Coxe or his master-builder must have known and admired the building, copying its dimensions in

the construction of Nether Lypiatt Manor. The theory was tested when the balcony was added: at the time Prince and Princess Michael moved in, they found that one first floor room – currently used as a drawing-room – had a door which opened on to the outside world and nothing but thin air. They therefore guessed that there must have been a balcony at one time, just as at Ashdown. So, following her hunch about the link between the two houses, Princess Michael asked the National Trust for details of the Ashdown Balcony. She then measured up at Nether Lypiatt – and found that a balcony modelled on Ashdown would fit perfectly, which thus strengthened her conviction over the relationship between the two homes.

The interior layout of Nether Lypiatt certainly does not bear a resemblance to Ashdown, however. Princess Michael, known for her expertise in interior design, describes what she found as 'rustic', adding that Judge Coxe 'either ran out of family money, or he was not a sophisticated man'. Seven new bathrooms have been installed, two serving the nursery on the top floor, three en-suite for bedrooms and two to serve the wings. Panelling, which was brown, has been lightened and the dining-room, which was too small and dark, has been enlarged, while the adjacent kitchen has been made smaller. Princess Michael notes, with regard to the latter, that rooms have obviously undergone changes of use throughout the years: a local lady once told her that she was actually born in what is now the kitchen! One enhancement which, sadly, was not made to the interior was the return of the seventeenth-century tapestries given to Gloucester College of Art by Anna Gordon. Two of these came up for auction at Sotheby's in 1982 when Gloucestershire County Council decided to sell them, but the Kents did not

Nearly all the rooms at Nether Lypiatt have stone bolection-moulded chimney-pieces, but that in the hall is of finely carved white and grey limestone

The balcony, modelled on that at Ashdown, fits perfectly, strengthening Princess Michael's conviction concerning the relationship between the two houses

get them back for the room in the manor for which they had originally been made!

Much work has been carried on in the grounds of the house to adapt outbuildings to meet the needs of a royal household. The dairy parlour, whose roof had collapsed, has been converted into a cottage, and the lofts over the stables have been converted into staff flats. A staff office and workshop has been accommodated in one barn and there are further plans to convert the large stone barn into a house for their son when he is older.

Leisure facilities have also been attended to: the swimming pool has been relined and the paving slabs which surrounded it have been taken up and replaced with York stone, which gives the whole area more character. The tennis court, adjacent to the pool, has been moved 11 feet and resurfaced. The Prince and Princess called in the En Tout Cas company to carry out this work and, remarkably, found that it was the very company which had laid the original court around 1919. Just as then, more bones were unearthed during the work, and again many thought they were the remains of soldiers killed in the Civil War, although others maintain that the skeletons would be older than that.

Nether Lypiatt Manor is a house of note, in terms of its architecture, its history and its mysteries which, from time to time, are illuminated by new discoveries. The question of the haunting is one which never fails to intrigue and the Kents themselves are frequently asked for their opinion. Princess Michael's answer is that 'every self-respecting old house should have spirits. We are very comfortable with them if they *are* there'. She adds: 'Animals are supposed to be sensitive to spirits and our cats and dogs are quite content. So if there *are* ghosts, they must be happy with us as the tenants.'

The Garden at Nether Lypiatt

BY ROSEMARY VEREY

This Grade I country house is once again being given a loved and well cared for garden. The approach road up the steep hill from Brimscombe is narrow – once it was a rough farm lane – so you must drive slowly to catch the first glimpse of this beautiful manor. On your right the perfectly designed wrought-iron gates and grilles with stone piers, made early in the eighteenth century for Judge Coxe, veil but do not conceal, enhancing the mystery, tantalizing the

In the front garden box-edged beds are planted entirely in blue, white and yellow

David Wynne's stag looks back across the terraced lawn to the knot garden and east face of the house

visitor. The house stands back only a short distance from the road.

Through the gates on this west side the inner courtyard has a pleasing symmetry. Either side of a straight stone path leading to the front door are pairs of box bushes clipped into tidy pyramids. Box-edged beds are filled with yellow 'Princess Michael of Kent' roses and with standard *R.* 'Iceberg' for extra height. The colour scheme for the west garden is entirely blue, white and yellow. Borders generously planted with shrubs and perennials outline the perimeter. The whole effect is one of dignity.

On the east side the new doorway from the dining-room takes you on to a broad stone terrace and then down steps to a lower lawn, where two knot patterns are laid out with scented herbs. From here the garden moves slowly down and away, with shrubs and a stag statue (by David Wynne), and then merges into the wonderful natural woodland.

'Princess Michael of Kent' roses in full, yellow bloom make a splash of colour

This is a garden for family activity. From the terrace and through a gate in the high stone wall you reach the swimming pool and tennis court, both surrounded by a mass of shrubs carefully chosen for scent and summer flowers and with trellis-work to disguise them. For many years old yew hedges have been an important feature in this garden, and the raised grass walk overlooking the court and pool has a fine example on one side; on the other, a lavender hedge tops the retaining wall.

This path leads into the woodland. Ten years ago this was full of brambles and nettles, now it is excitingly planted with buddleias, viburnums, philadelphus, choisyas, lilacs, all acting as understorey for the high canopy of woodland trees. More light has been let in and new bulbs are naturalizing, while those of past generations have become revitalized.

The great and wonderful drama is the long avenue of lime trees with tall straight trunks and branches interlacing overhead. It is like a majestic cathedral aisle, stately and full of promise in winter, beautiful in spring when the young leaves are opening and the carpet of bulbs unrolls, and cool and luxuriant in its summer dress. Here there are bluebells, daffodils and narcissus, snowdrops, cyclamen and alliums. Walk the full length of this silent avenue before you turn around and you will see the house as a jewel framed by the grandeur of nature.

There is much more to see: a prolific fruit cage, greenhouses for tender plants and cuttings, frames for propagating and hardening young seedlings. Lilies, scented geraniums, daturas and fuchsias await their turn to be brought into the house or stood on the terrace.

An old apple tunnel is lovely in blossom in springtime,

The lime avenue, with its interlacing branches, resembles a majestic cathedral

The rose maze, its complex paths presenting a medley of colour, even in late summer

and beside it in 1986 Princess Michael planted her rose maze. The narrow beds are in the shape of ever-decreasing squares; they are an amazing medley of colour in the summer, when picking and dead-heading are high on the list of daily jobs. The prevailing wind is south-west, blowing the scent of roses to the house.

As you finish the tour of the garden you can pass the herb garden, descend some stone steps and turn back towards the house into a small enclosed secret garden, where Princess Michael limits the colour to just green, with white and black flowers for drama.

This garden is a perfect complement in its structure of formality and woodland to the elegant and much loved William and Mary house.

Acknowledgements

Original text by Geoffrey Sanders with architectural notes by David Verey; further information researched and written by Siân Ellis.

The publisher would like to thank the following for help in providing information: Fred Cook, Tetbury; Nick Mould, Deputy Land Steward of the Duchy of Cornwall's East District; Terry Summers, Farm Director, Duchy of Cornwall; David Fisher, Nether Lypiatt; Peter Harding, Tetbury; Stan Gardiner, France Lynch; H.R.H. Princess Michael of Kent; Ted Prince, Tetbury.

Picture Credits

All colour photography by Paul Felix unless otherwise stated. Other illustrations:

Nic Barlow, 109, 118, 121, 122, 125; Ed Buziac, 75; Jack Farley, 37; Fitzwilliam Museum, Cambridge, 69 (top); Stan Gardiner, 43 (top), 68, 79, 83, 84, 96 (bottom), 97 (top), 103, 107, 111, 112; Gloucestershire County Library, 26, 28, 72, 95; Gloucestershire Record Office, 22 (top); Tim Graham Picture Library, 6; Richard Greenly Photography/Duchy of

Cornwall, 53; Peter Harding, 44, 47; Martin Latham, 63; S.G. Mosdell, 39; National Monuments Record, Crown Copyright, 101, 110, 119; National Portrait Gallery Archives, 74; Ted Prince, 27 (bottom), 31; R. Sollars, 106; Davina Wynne-Jones, Gryffon Press, 21.